Pastor Sal's Ser
YouTube Channel.
" Cumberland County Community Church"

The Goodness and Wonders of The Lord
Sal Roggio

This book is dedicated to the churches I have been privileged to serve in and the people of God I served with.

Contents

Introduction	V
1. Proclaim His Wondrous Deeds	1
2. The Presence of God	5
3. Convinced	10
4. Take All The Shop Classes You Can	15
5. Nancy	19
6. The Military	23
7. The Journey Begins	29
8. Confirmation	34
9. Obstacles	40
10. Power From On High	45
11. The Next Step	50
12. Learning To Ask	54
13. He Is Able To Do Above All We Ask Or Think	58

14.	Deliverance From The Demonic	63
15.	A Reason To Rejoice	68
16.	A Divine Appointment	73
17.	Pastor, Do You Have A Need?	78
18.	Who Will Set Me Free?	83
19.	Tammy	89
20.	Ordination	94
21.	Mr. Sunday School	99
22.	My God Is Bigger Than That	105
23.	You Gotta Your Permits	109
24.	Mountain Moving Faith	113
25.	A Drive In The Snow	118
26.	The Holy Spirit	123
27.	Never Forsaken	127
28.	A Title Deed From God	133
29.	The Reality Of Humanity	138
30.	The 911 Call	142
31.	Prayer and Proclamation	146

Introduction

   Sal Roggio has been active in ministry for over 50 years. More than forty of those have been as a senior pastor. He is currently pastor of Cumberland County Community Church in Millville, New Jersey. As founding pastor, he has served there since 1987. He graduated from the Moody Bible Institute in 1977 with a degree in Pastoral Ministries and received a bachelor's degree from Trinity Christian College in 1979. Sal has been married to his wife Nancy since 1971. They have four grown daughters.
   In this his first book, he has written a devotional. It contains thirty-one days of actual accounts that demonstrate the ever presence of God in the believer's life. The book begins with an account of when he was two years old and badly beaten. It is his conviction that every Christian can look back on life and recall the Goodness of God. He wrote this 31 day devotional to encourage members of his congregation that God often gives evidence of His presence, love, and care. Most of the accounts are about the first half of his life. He soon found, as he reflected on God's involvement in his life, there were far too events to cover in a thirty-one

day devotional. With that in mind he has expressed a desire to tell the more of the story in a second devotional.

Copyright © 2024 by Salvatore Roggio
All rights reserved.
No portion of this book may be reproduced in any form without written permission from the publisher or author, except as permitted by U.S. copyright law.

All Scripture verses are from the English Standard Version unless otherwise indicated.

You can find more information about Cumberland County Community Church at ccccmillville.org

Chapter 1
Proclaim His Wondrous Deeds

> O God, from my youth you have taught me, and I still proclaim your wondrous deeds. So even to old age and gray hairs, O God, do not forsake me, until I proclaim your might to another generation, your power to all those to come (Psalms 71:17-18)

I discovered this article on the internet over twenty-five years ago. I will explain its importance to me at the end.

Reunited After 25 Years
"This story is a positive end to a negative beginning. The author of this article prefers to remain anonymous in order to protect innocent family members. As the story unfolds, it is exciting to see the part technology, and the internet play in aiding the happy reuniting of brothers. As the result of a family tragedy, two young brothers, ages two years, and three years, are hospitalized after a brutal beating. A young sister who is five years old stands helplessly watching, unable to come to the aid of her brothers.

Shortly after this horrible event, the brothers are released from the hospital and a court hearing is held. The three children, whom we will call Larry, Steve and Darlene are removed from their home and put into an orphanage. The result is the loss of sibling camaraderie that is normally experienced and Darlene rarely sees her brothers as she is housed in a building away from theirs.

The children grow up and go their separate ways. Darlene and Larry become drifters and traverse the countryside. Steve, the youngest is the most stable and settles down in the area closest to family members. Although Darlene does manage an occasional visit with Larry or Steve when they find her or she finds them, Larry and Steve lose contact and do not see or hear from each other for more than twenty years.

Through the Internet, Darlene is able to locate Larry, and put him in contact with Steve. Imagine Darlene's joy when all three carry on a live three way phone conversation through Fire Talk (an Internet messaging service). The three of them had not been together in any type of situation for over twenty years. Darlene was brought to tears experiencing the kinship with brothers she had missed as a child.

As a result of getting the two brothers together, they were able to reunite and Steve went to visit Larry recently. They all keep in touch now through email and Fire talk and now in their fifties are able to develop the sibling relationship that they were unable to experience as children. Darlene, Steve and Larry all live in different parts of the country, however with modern technology and the Internet are now able to share business ventures."

As I read the story I myself began to tear up. Though the names were different I remember the events with clarity. After a little research I discovered the story had been penned by my sister. The three children, Darlene, Larry and Steve were in effect, Doran, Louis, and Sal. I was two years old when the event took place. I believe it was that event that set the stage in my life to discover my need of a Saviour.

God told the prophet Jeremiah, "Before I formed you in the womb I knew you..." (Jeremiah 1:5). I may not have known that truth when the above event took place, but I am confident about God's involvement in my life. This devotional will tell some of the stories of how God revealed " wondrous deeds" to me in the 70 years since this event occurred. Perhaps if this is well received I will share in another devotional some of the more personal struggles and of experiencing God's grace. I thank God he has allowed me to live to "old age and gray hairs" so that I might "proclaim His might to another generation".

Lord, I pray that the events shared in this brief devotional might be used by you in this generation. Thank you that in the brokenness of early life I was led to my Saviour and Lord, Jesus Christ.

Thought: Take time to reflect on your life and think about the incident or point in time when you realized your need of God. Thank Him for that event that exposed that need.

PERSONAL REFLECTION:

Chapter 2
The Presence of God

> God is our refuge and strength, a very present help in trouble. Therefore will not we fear, though the earth be removed, and though the mountains be carried into the midst of the sea; Though the waters thereof roar and be troubled, though the mountains shake with the swelling thereof.
> (Psalms 46:1-3 KJV)

Shortly after the beating I experienced as mentioned in day one I found myself in a homeless shelter, then a Catholic home for children, then finally I ended up in the Baptist Home for Children. The sequence is hard to remember since I was 2 years old when these events started. Out of the three places the bulk of my time was spent in the Baptist Home. I see this as the hand of God in my life.

When I arrived at the home they placed me in a dormitory with older boys. There was no facility for children my age. I would spend time with the house mother during the day as I was too young for school. I remember taking trips on the trolly or bus to visit some of her family or friends in Philadelphia. When I could not be with her during the day I spent time in the home of the orphanage director. He was an ordained minister and he and his wife treated me kindly. That was my first real influence toward the knowledge of God.

Every Sunday we all attended a church service. I do not remember going to Sunday School but remember we were to sit quietly in the pew and listen to the preacher. Upon returning to the dormitory we would be served lunch then would be required to sit still in the living room area for a couple of hours to honor the Lord's Day.

The campus had a chapel, and the children did special programs. Nothing comes to my mind but one singular event. We were all required to memorize Psalms 46 and recite it publicly as a group to the other children. What is amazing is how the first three verses have encouraged and guided me through the years. In those days, the only translation we had was the KJV so here is what I remembered.

"God is our refuge and strength, a very present help in trouble. Therefore we will not fear, though the earth be removed, and though the mountains be carried into the midst of the sea; Though the waters thereof roar and be troubled, though the mountains shake with the swelling thereof" (Psalm 46:1-3 KJV).

The end of the chapter has also brought great comfort as life's twist and turns hit me. This I was learning, and now know with certainty, that God was with me. His words still give me assurance

> "Be still and know that I am God: I will be exalted among the heathen, I will be exalted in the earth. The LORD of hosts is with us; the God of Jacob is our refuge"
> (Psalms 46:10-11 KJV).

In the pages ahead you will see the faithfulness of God unfold. It is now about 72 years since that brutal day. I hope that the stories of God's good hand in my life will be an encouragement to you and that you will surely know that "our Lord is truly a very present help in trouble."

Dear Lord, I am thankful for your continual faithfulness. I have known your presence in my life now for many years. You have truly been my refuge and strength! Grant to all who read this the calmness that comes from knowing that you are God, and a very present help in trouble.

Thought: Reflect upon a time when God met you in your distress. Consider what he has brought you through. Give thanks knowing He cares for you. How might you share your story of God's great grace with someone who needs to be reminded that, "The LORD is near to all who call on him," (Psalms 145:18).

PERSONAL REFLECTION:

The Baptist Home for Children. The building on the upper right was where I stayed. I do not know where my siblings lived because we rarely saw each other unless someone came to visit us.

A visit from our grandmother near the end of our stay at The Baptist Home for Children. From left to right, Louis, Sal, and Doran.

CHAPTER 3
CONVINCED

> **And they were bringing children to him that he might touch them, and the disciples rebuked them. But when Jesus saw it, he was indignant and said to them, "Let the children come to me; do not hinder them, for to such belongs the kingdom of God."**
> **(Mark 10:13-14)**

> **Come, O children, listen to me; I will teach you the fear of the LORD.**
> **(Psalms 34:11)**

When I was about seven years old, I went to live with my father and stepmother. That put me in a place where I would have three other exposures to the Gospel. The first was at North Wales Baptist Church. I attended Sunday School, and Vacation Bible School. It was also through the church ministry I attended a summer camp. I am sure I heard the gospel in those settings. Each played a role in my life. But there were two other events that were pivotal in discovering Christ as Saviour.

One was my father's influence. My father had been part of a popular singing group called the Four Chimes. He was a world class guitar player. Often, he would play hymns on his guitar and sing. I still remember two of his favorites. "In the Garden" and "Love lifted Me." We often joined in on the chorus;

Love lifted me! Love lifted me!

When nothing else could help

Love lifted me!

At that time I attended the Towamencin Elementary School. Things were different in those days. During recess we were permitted to go to a house across the street. We were taken to a garage where a lady told flannel graft Bible stories. I loved hearing the stories. Each week we were challenged to memorize Bible verses. There I learned the first twelve verses of the Gospel of John. Everyone was given a little prize when we memorized verses. I was highly motivated. I am sure the invitation to invite Christ into my heart was given and I did. But it was not until later in life that I knew I believed. This is how it happened.

My mother remarried and we all went to live with her. Church was not part of our life at that time.

Living in the Kensington area of Philadelphia I soon was hanging out with other boys my age. Often, we found ourselves walking the streets of Philly. One day we were hanging together near the railroad tracks and one of the boys began to mock God in the conversation. Soon others joined in. All of a sudden, I felt my temperature rising. Suddenly I blurted out, "You can't talk about God that way!" I was as shocked as they were. My hand went to my forehead as I said to myself, "You really believe this." It was at that moment I knew that I believed in my heart and confessed with my mouth.

The truth of the scriptures became a reality in my life that day. We are told *"if you confess with your mouth that Jesus is Lord and believe in your heart that God raised him from the dead, you will be saved. For with the heart one believes and is justified, and with the mouth one confesses and is saved"* (Romans 10:9-10).

As a pastor, often people come to me when we are planning a baptismal service asking if they could be baptized a second time. They tell me they heard about receiving Jesus as Saviour when they were young and were baptized. Now they are not sure they fully understood what is meant to commit their life to Him. When they ask, I never hesitate to say yes. I know just what they mean. I am only glad that now our hearts are certain. To God be the glory.

> *Dear Lord, thank you for those who when we were young told us about the love of Jesus. Thank you that there came a time that we knew without doubt that we had committed our all to Him. May all who read this account, know with certainty, that they have put their faith in the Lord, and are able to confess that faith before others.*

Thought: Are you utterly convinced that Jesus is Lord? How do you feel when you overhear someone mock those who believe in Christ? Are you willing to be identified with Jesus as your Lord and Saviour regardless of what anyone says? Do you wish they knew him as you do? Take a moment and give God thanks for the assurance of your salvation.

If you do not have the assurance that Jesus Christ is your Lord and Saviour now is the perfect time to settle that issue. The word of God is clear when it states "Everyone who calls on the name of the Lord will be saved." You are included in that promise.

Personal Reflection:

North Wales Baptist Church

Chapter 4
Take All The Shop Classes You Can

> **The heart of man plans his way, but the LORD establishes his steps.
> (Proverbs 16:9)**

Junior High came quickly. It was a new world to me. We had choices in our courses. I was not an honor student or a high academic achiever. I didn't know what to do. The answer came rapidly though when I met with a school counselor. I'm sure he meant the best for me. He told me I probably would not do well in the academic classes. He suggested if I wanted to be able to support a family someday that I should take all the shop classes I could. I was ok with that. I liked working with my hands. Both my father and stepfather worked in factories. I thought I would follow in their footsteps.

After graduating from Stetson Jr. High, I heard of a special school in Philadelphia called The Philadelphia High School of Agriculture & Horticulture. Stetson was a tough intercity school. When I found out about this school of about 300 students at the outskirts of the city I applied and was accepted. Again I was not in the academic class but what they called industrial arts. I thought I might like to be a veterinarian but soon discovered I could not spell or pronounce the words. By the time I graduated I was not sure what I would be doing. About two weeks after graduation I was in boot camp. My father had been in the Navy and I would follow in his steps. The Navy sent me to electrician's school.

Of course God knew my future. He knew one day I would enter the ministry. Ever since I became a full time pastor I have been involved in building projects. When I pastored in Sauk Village Illinois the church began to grow and we added three mobile classrooms. The miraculous hand of God can clearly be seen in that project. We will recall some of the marvelous events that happened in future devotions.

Since starting the Cumberland County Community Church in 1987 we have been building. When I went into the ministry I had no idea God would use me to not only reach people with the gospel but that I would be involved in so much construction. In five years of college to prepare for the ministry I was not taught about building projects. It never occurred to me how important facilities are until I experienced the lack of space in Illinois. But I was being prepared long before I found myself having to oversee the construction of church projects. It is wonderful to look back at life and see the truth of God's word.

> **"The steps of a man are established by the LORD, when he delights in his way;" (Psalms 37:23).**

Year by year I have witnessed the mighty hand of God. Isn't it amazing how the Lord equips us with His gifts and uses our life's circumstances so we might be productive for Him. God wastes nothing, not even your struggles and disappointments. All these are used by Him to equip you for service.

> *Dear Lord, thank you for never taking your hand off of me. Through times of loss and disappointment you were preparing me for your glory. You directed and redirected according to your good will. You showed me you were willing to use all who worship you. Thank you for your guiding hand.*

Thought: Have you ever considered how you got where you are today. Can you look back and see how God opened one door and closed another. Have you thought about how God will use you for His glory, using your strengths and weaknesses? Give Him thanks that as you look back at life you can see how your steps were ordered by the Lord.

Personal Reflection:

CHAPTER 5

NANCY

> **An excellent wife who can find? She is far more precious than jewels. The heart of her husband trusts in her, and he will have no lack of gain. She does him good, and not harm, all the days of her life.**
> **(Proverbs 31:10-12)**

I remember the time I first met my wife. I was sitting in class in the Agricultural school and the teacher asked for a volunteer to show a family with two prospective students the campus. I raised my hand and was chosen for the task. That's when I met Nancy and her family. I took them on the tour and it looked like they wanted to attend the school. As they were leaving, I mentioned to one of the other students, "I just met the girl I'm going to marry." The rest is history. Now married over fifty-two years I can say I am glad I met Nancy.

When she arrived at the school I would sit at her table for lunch. That was about the only time of the day I saw her since she was in the academic class and I was in the industrial arts class. Almost daily during the school week, I was at the table telling her exaggerated stories about myself. It's a wonder she listened. I developed a strategy for going to her house, by going to see her brother and work on our cars. I think we went on a couple of double dates and soon I was a regular at her home. I usually only made it there on Sunday's. The trip from my house was about 18 miles.

Looking back, it is easy to see the hand of God working in our lives. Nancy attended the Olney Baptist Church each Sunday. I hadn't been attending anywhere. She invited me to go with her. I would drive to her house and we would walk together the block and a half to the church. After the service we would go to her home for dinner. In the evening we attended the youth group which was a part of a movement called Christian Endeavor. Often the leaders of the group would give us a topic and assign two people to give a pro or con talk on it. I soon found myself taking part in the discussion. It forced me to think through issues using the Bible.

The impact was great. It was clear I was growing in faith. When I graduated school and was preparing to go into the Navy, Nancy gave me a New Scofield Reference Bible. I took it with me. I read it and found the notes helpful. She and I were not aware that God would one day call me into full time service. I look back and thank Him for bringing into my life a woman of God who would one day join me in ministry. **The Bible says, "An excellent wife is the crown of her husband..." (Proverbs 12:4).** To that I can say amen.

Paul says some are called to serve the Lord as single. He says that "I want you to be free from anxieties. **The unmarried man is anxious about the things of the Lord, how to please the Lord. But the married man is anxious about worldly things, how to please his wife," (1 Corinthians 7:32-33).** I can honestly say my wife has been with me every step of the way.

> *Dear Lord, thank you for bringing into my life a woman who would not only love me but also be an example of a woman of God. I pray for the marriages of each one reading this account that they too would experience oneness in Christ with their marriage partners. May they in surrendering to you experience the "one flesh relationship" of Ephesians 5:31. I pray also for those who are not married but serve you fully. In whatever setting we find ourselves in, let us be serving the Lord.*

Thought: Oneness comes when two people share the same values. There is an old saying that opposites attract. In reality when it comes to oneness in marriage or any other relationship the truth is that similarity produces harmony. It is good to be reminded of the word from the prophet, "Do two walk together, unless they have agreed to meet?" (Amos 3:3). That works in marriage and also in the body of Christ. Let us all work "to maintain the unity of the Spirit in the bond of peace" (Ephesians 4:3).

Personal Reflection:

Chapter 6
The Military

> **All the ways of a man are pure in his own eyes, but the LORD weighs the spirit. Commit your work to the LORD, and your plans will be established.**
> **(Proverbs 16:2-5)**

Right after High school I joined the Navy. Little did I know how the years in the children's home's had prepared me for life in the service. While boot camp had challenges, one thing I had little trouble with was taking orders. In the children's homes, both the Catholic one and the Baptist one we were taught to respond to authority and take orders. Yes ma'am and no sir were how we were to speak to those who had charge over us. We were required to make our bed and to be up at a certain time and our day was regulated by the schedule we were given.

When I joined the service it was not much different. This served me well in boot camp. Often men would get demerits or had to drop down and do pushups or some other action for not bring on par with the demands made upon them. I remember the discipline received in the homes and knew that when given an order or instruction I was to obey it. I don't remember being disciplined for anything. I understood authority.

Having completed bootcamp and electrical school I was stationed on the USS Donner LSD 20. I began to go through the ranks very quickly. I was engaged to Nancy at the time and apart from some sightseeing had little need to go off the ship. I started studying the manuals to prepare me to take the test for the next rank and in a very short time became an E5. I had gained the respect of my superior officers as one who could be relied upon.

It was at that time the Navy came up with a strange idea. Our ship was mostly DC current with a few exceptions for some advanced equipment that was powered by an AC generator. We received a directive that the ship was going to be converted to fluorescent lighting. No one was sure why but nonetheless we followed orders. It turned out to be a real nightmare. Fluorescents in those days had starters that when energized would provide the spark that would light the bulbs. After a couple of starts the starter would burn out and the bulbs would not light. Much of the ship would go dark.

This was serious and we soon were without starters. It became a genuine hazard and out at sea we did not have the resources to correct the situation. Something had to be done. Until we could replace the faulty system we devised a method of restarting the lights. We would pull the starters out and take two narrow screwdrivers, place them into the two holes the starters screwed into, then cross the screwdrivers to create an electric current that would light the bulbs.

This was no easy task and could prove to be dangerous. The ship would rock and we had to find a way to get to the lights since they were overhead. It would not take much to get an electrical shock. Speed was important and it was tiring. But we kept at it. As soon as possible we found a way to correct the problem. It lingered for a long time, and it was like being on alert constantly.

Shortly after we got things under control I was ordered to the upper deck on the bow of the ship in full uniform. The captain was having a ceremony and I was to be there. I had been to these kinds of ceremonies before. Some were where a sailor had stepped out of line and the captain pronounced a judgment. Often a sailor forfeited a rank. I was told my event was to be positive.

Once on deck I was called to go before the captain. There to my surprise I received a citation for the work I had done keeping lights working on the ship. It didn't seem like something you get a citation for. I felt I was doing my job. It was what I signed up for. But I discovered on that day that the attitude and skill you bring to a job matters.

The Lord is looking for faithfulness in each one of us. When we became believers we may not have realized it but we enlisted. The scriptures sometimes refers to believers as "soldiers" (2 Timothy 2:3-4).

One day we will be called front and center and our works will be manifest. I pray for each one of us that that day we will hear from our Lord, "Well done, good and faithful servant. You have been faithful over a little; I will set you over much. Enter into the joy of your master" (Matthew 25:21).

Dear Lord, remind us that what we do and how we do things in life matters. As the word tells us "For we must all appear before the judgment seat of Christ, so that each one may receive what is due for what he has done in the body, whether good or evil (2 Corinthians 5:10). Let us serve with devotion to our duty that flows out of our love for the saviour. Let us seek the reward that comes from faithful service (1 Corinthians 3:13).

Thought: Scripture tells us, "Whatever you do, work heartily, as for the Lord and not for men, knowing that from the Lord you will receive the inheritance as your reward. You are serving the Lord Christ" (Colossians 3:23-24). It is amazing how you are able to go above and beyond when you realize what you do matters not only for now but for eternity. Ask God to grant you a servant's heart and you will be surprised how much lighter your load becomes.

Personal Reflection:

```
                                                    9 May 1970

From:   Commanding Officer, USS DONNER (LSD-20)
To:     EM2 Salvatore W. ROGGIO, USN, B41 45 71

Subj:   Commendation

1.  The Commanding Officer, USS DONNER (LSD-20), takes great pleasure
in commending you for exceptional performance as set forth in the follow-
ing citation:

        During the period 1 May 1969, to 9 May 1970, your professional
        performance, military behavior and devotion to duty have been
        exemplary.  In order to improve the ship and her equipment you
        have consistently worked long hours, many of which have been
        during the time which you rated liberty or other off-duty time.
        You have made a significant contribution to DONNER's high state
        of readiness, both materially and operationally, enabling her
        to meet all commitments while deployed to the Sixth Fleet from
        July to December 1969, during the complex and demanding Spring
        board Operation in February and March 1970, and during Operation
        Exotic Dancer III in May 1970.  Your alert and responsive
        performance of duty has been in keeping with the highest
        traditions of the United States Navy.


                                        R. W. MALONE

Copy to:
Service Record
```

Navy Commendation

Chapter 7

The Journey Begins

> **The steps of a man are established by the LORD, when he delights in his way; (Psalms 37:23)**

In 1973 I was a washing machine repair man servicing coin operated equipment in apartments and other laundry areas such as college campuses. We were living in Philadelphia at the time. The owner's brother operated the same kind of repair business in New Jersey. As his brother was nearing retirement he sold his business to my boss. Now he was looking for an employee to work the New Jersey route. A number of years earlier while dating Nancy, we had seen an add on TV about land being sold in Laurel Lake, New Jersey. We thought that investing in property might be a wise move, so we drove down and purchased a piece of land. I informed my boss I had property in New Jersey and was willing to move. However, I told him I didn't have the ability to finance developing the property and put a mobile home on it. He said he would finance the project to make the move possible. The deal was struck.

At that time Nancy and I were serving as youth workers in the Olney Baptist Church in Philadelphia. A short time before this opportunity, I had gone with our youth on a retreat. At the close of the weekend an invitation was given for people not only to come to know Jesus Christ as Saviour, but also to consider committing to a life of service. I shared later with Nancy that I felt God was calling me to full time ministry but had no idea how to go about it.

We moved to New Jersey and quickly got involved in a local church. That church was the Central Baptist in Millville where John DenBleyker pastored. John was a man full of grace and we soon became friends. It wasn't long before I was serving in the church. Knowing my heart and desire to be used by God, Pastor DenBleyker invited me to lead the congregation in prayer on Sundays. I also helped in the Sunday School. They had a high energy young couples ministry that Nancy and I became involved in.

Servicing laundry equipment had me on the road for many hours. I found a Christian radio station, WKDN, 106.9 FM, of Camden, and kept it on most of the time while in my service van. One day when working in Camden I decided to check out the station. It was there that I met a kindhearted believer named John Zesewitz. John was the chief engineer and when he heard of my desire to become a pastor he told me about Moody Bible

Institute. He and his wife Elaine had graduated from there and their enthusiasm for the school spilled over into me. They also encouraged Nancy with stories of the ministry they had for married student's wives. I applied and by God's grace was accepted.

When I mentioned the school to pastor DenBleyker he said he had been wanting to go to one of their pastors' conferences. Knowing I planned to move out there in the fall he invited me to go with him to attend the event. That was great because I needed to find a place for us to live. We registered for the conference and drove out to Chicago, Illinois. I had never been on a Christian college campus before but instantly fell in love with the school.

After we had spent a day there, we looked up the Dean of Students. I told him I was coming for the fall semester and needed to find a place to live. He told me he was sorry but was unaware of any places that were available. A little discouraged, I went back to the conference where we heard more messages about our great God. I was hopeful and sure God would provide our need. After a great night of sermons, singing, and fellowship we headed to our dorm room. When we approached the door there was a note from the Dean. Someone had called and an apartment had become available.

The next morning, we connected with the dean. He told us that someone had called the school and was looking for a fall student who needed an apartment. In exchange for cleaning the church, and doing other maintenance tasks, they would provide a two bedroom apartment. The apartment was directly under the parsonage which was attached to the church itself. It could not be more convenient. How excited I was and I anxiously waited for a break in the conference schedule so we could go investigate this opportunity. That afternoon we met pastor Don Harrison, of the Temple Baptist Church, and his wife Ruth. He showed us the place and it was more than adequate for our needs. We were ready to move.

> *Dear Lord, how thankful we are that you lead us into green pastures. You say, "The steps of a man are established by the Lord , when he delights in his way", (Psalms 37:23). I have been overwhelmed by the way we have been directed. May the memory of this journey make us forever aware that you hold our hand every step of the way.*

Thought: Hebrews 11 tells of saints that stepped out in faith. They did not always know where they were going but they knew who was going with them. Have you come to understand that the Lord we serve has said, "I will never leave you nor forsake you" (Hebrews 13:5). Are you ready to take the next step of Faith?

Personal Reflection:

Central Baptist Church
Millville N.J.

Chapter 8
Confirmation

> **But Moses said to the LORD, "Oh, my Lord, I am not eloquent, either in the past or since you have spoken to your servant, but I am slow of speech and of tongue." Then the LORD said to him, "Who has made man's mouth? Who makes him mute, or deaf, or seeing, or blind? Is it not I, the LORD? Now therefore go, and I will be with your mouth and teach you what you shall speak."**
> **(Exodus 4:10-12)**

About the time I felt called to full time ministry my employer enrolled me in a Dale Carnegie Seminar. He felt he had seen some potential in me, and might be considering me for a different position in the company. I had no idea what the seminar was about, but soon found out it included a lot of public speaking. Little did I know the Lord was bringing me through another step of preparation.

The first or second week at the class I met another participant and in our conversation we discovered we were both Christians. He challenged me to make an agreement with him that whenever we got up to speak, we would use our talk to share our faith with the class. I took the challenge, and I was soon surprised how the Lord would use me. The class was filled with talented individuals from many kinds of professions, and I am reasonably sure I was the only repairman in the class.

One week I spoke on being ready to meet God. One of the men who attended the class that week disappeared until the course was nearly over. He was a successful businessman who owned a chain of popular girls' clothing stores. When he did come back to the class, he made it a point to catch up with me. He told me he had gone to the hospital with a serious heart issue. As he was being rushed to the hospital, he kept asking himself if he was ready to meet God. I was startled to know that God had used my talk to cause this man to consider eternal issues.

It was not long after the two of us shared our faith that others in the class began talking about spiritual things. It felt like a mini revival was taking place in the seminar. One night after class I stepped out of the building and started walking to my car. It was raining and I was moving briskly. I heard a yell behind me. One of the students was running after me. As he approached me, I heard him cry out, "Sal I don't know what it is you've got, but I've got to get it." There in the pouring rain I had the privilege of sharing about faith in the Lord Jesus Christ.

Each session we were given a topic to speak about. The subject would not be known until we arrived at the class. One week we were asked to give a talk on, "How to Control Worry and Reduce Tension." When it came time to go before the class and speak, I told the story of the Israelites traveling through the wilderness and how God provided for all their needs by giving them water and manna and seeing that their clothes did not wear out. After everyone had spoken the class would take a vote and choose who they felt gave the best talk. That week the vote went to me. I was presented with a book written by Dorothy Carnegie titled "Don't Grow Old-Grow Up!"

A wonderful thing happened during that course. The Lord confirmed in my heart that He would be pleased to use me. I was encouraged and motivated to step out in faith as we made plans to move to Chicago, but there were some obstacles to overcome. We will look at them tomorrow.

> *Dear Lord, remind us that you spoke to Moses and said, "Who has made man's mouth?...Now therefore go, and I will be with your mouth and teach you what you shall speak." Let us be willing to step out in faith to whatever task you call us to do. Startle us with wonder that you use ordinary people to do your work. May someone want to know what we have, and may we be able to tell that we have a Saviour, Jesus Christ the Lord.*

Thought: Have ever felt like you had nothing to offer God? Would you like to be surprised by His divine enablement? Make a commitment to speak about Him. Ask what situation God has put you in that would give you a chance to speak of His greatness. Pray with someone that you both would speak up, and then get together to share what God has done. Be encouraged, God will use you.

Personal Reflection:

DON'T GROW OLD—GROW UP!

by DOROTHY CARNEGIE
PRESIDENT, DALE CARNEGIE and ASSOCIATES, Inc

The book embodying the advice which has helped thousands in the world-famous courses given by the DALE CARNEGIE INSTITUTE. Covers such provocative topics as:

- THE FIRST STEP TOWARDS MATURITY — RESPONSIBILITY
- ACTION IS FOR ADULTS
- MATURITY OF SPIRIT
- MARRIAGE IS FOR GROWNUPS
- MATURITY AND MAKING FRIENDS
- HOW OLD ARE YOU?
- THREE GREAT RULES FOR MENTAL HEALTH: KNOW YOURSELF, LIKE YOURSELF, BE YOURSELF

DON'T GROW OLD—

GROW UP!

This book has been presented by a vote of Dale Carnegie Course Class Number 7-304 to SAL ROGGIO on the 3 day of May, 19 73 for a memorable talk on "How to Control Worry and Reduce Tension."

Congratulations!

Dorothy Carnegie

CHAPTER 9
OBSTACLES

> **If any of you lacks wisdom, let him ask God, who gives generously to all without reproach, and it will be given to him. But let him ask in faith, with no doubting, for the one who doubts is like a wave of the sea that is driven and tossed by the wind. For that person must not suppose that he will receive anything from the Lord; he is a double-minded man, unstable in all his ways.**
> **(James 1:5-8)**

The experience of attending the Dale Carnegie Seminar encouraged me in my call into full time service. It also presented a problem. My employer was investing a good amount of money in me. After a few weeks I began to feel uneasy about that arrangement. It was clear that my boss was expecting to get a return on his investment. I did not want to be thoughtless, receive this training and simply resign if I were accepted into Bible School. I felt I owed him an explanation. So I went to see Mr. Cooper, the owner of the company.

" Mr. Cooper, I came to talk to you about my situation", I said. "I know you are making an investment in me. I have been sensing in my heart a call from God to go to college and study to be a pastor. I wanted you to know because I didn't want you to put out the expense of my continuing in the Dale Carnegie Class when there might be a chance by the fall of this year, I will be leaving the company to attend Bible school." I let him know that at that time I was not yet accepted but that was my intent. His response surprised me.

Mr. Cooper said it was his desire to send me to the course. He asked if I thought he could afford the cost. I replied "yes" because I knew he was well off. He asked if he could spend his money as he chose. Again, I agreed. "Well," he said, "I want you to finish the course." "Yes sir" I said. I would if he so wished. Then something unusual happened. He called his brother Morris into the room. This was the brother he bought the New Jersey coin operated laundry equipment route from.

When Morris entered the room Mr. Cooper told him what I had said about my intentions. He told his brother that he planned to change my mind. Next, he made a wager in front of me. He bet his brother a hundred dollars he would change my mind and I would stay with the company. In another conversation he told me of his children being doctors and lawyers and having no need of his business when he retired. The impression he gave was that if I stayed with the company I might be in line to get a piece of it. That was a moment of testing. Did God really call me into full time service? I was serving Him now in the church I was attending, but I knew in my heart I was going to go to Bible college. I had just one more obstacle.

It was Mr. Cooper who financed our mobile home when he bought his brother's business. He realized that I would not leave his employment owing him money. But as I had been discovering, obstacles are opportunities for God to reveal his glory. As I prayed about the situation, I also mentioned the dilemma to my father. My father said he had an idea. He said he would talk to my Uncle Victor who owned the company dad worked for and see what could be done. Uncle Victor's factory was highly successful and employed a great many people. My uncle called the bank that the company dealt with and mentioned my need.

In a couple of days the bank called me and asked some pertinent questions. A day or two later the bank called again and said my loan was ready. I could come in and pick up the check. Mr. Cooper got his money, and I was free from my obligations. Soon after, I received my acceptance letter for Moody Bible Institute. I gave my notice to the company and started to plan the move. Mr. Cooper called me into his office. After chatting about my plans he made a startling remark to me. He told me he did not believe in God before I became his employee, but he did believe there was a God now. On my last day at work there was a note for me. It was a note from

Mr. Cooper thanking me for working for him. Inside was a hundred dollars.

> *Dear Lord, thank you for the ways you prove us. You help us to understand the commitment of our hearts. Thank you for the way you reveal to us that obstacles expose your glory. Thank you also for memories that we can think upon in difficult days and be reminded that you have guided us every step of the way. Thank you that when we are faithful to you, we touch the lives of others who need you.*

Thought: Many times the Lord gives us an uphill road to travel as we move forward in obeying his will for our life. He wants us to realize it is He who leads, guides, and directs servants. He also is preparing us for the road ahead. Often in life we face obstacles. God in His grace gives us memories of His past involvement in our lives, so we reflect on His provisions, we discover we have strength for the Journey. Praise God for His faithfulness.

Personal Reflection:

Chapter 10
Power From On High

> **Now to him who is able to do far more abundantly than all that we ask or think, according to the power at work within us, to him be glory in the church and in Christ Jesus throughout all generations, forever and ever. Amen.**
> **(Ephesians 3:20-21)**

Having been accepted as a student at Moody Bible Institute we began the trip. It was Nancy, our daughter Susan and me. That was the first major trip we would take as a family. We were filled with excitement. Our mobile home went up for sale and we began to pack. It was 1974 and the economy was bad. As a result, the home didn't sell. Later we would discover that that was divine providence. As for now we found some renters and made our way to Chicago.

Living in the Humboldt Park area of Chicago had some challenges. We moved into our basement apartment under the parsonage. It was more than adequate. It had a small concrete yard that was filled with broken glass. We quickly cleaned it up. The kitchen windows faced the side alley and we soon learned that when it rained we needed to be sure they were closed. If they weren't when a car drove down the alleyway water would splash onto our sink and dish rack. Nonetheless it was home and a provision from the Lord.

Our first week there we were shopping at a supermarket about a block and a half from the church. While there our car was broken into. That was when we discovered that we were a block away from an apartment complex that was mostly under control of the "Latin Kings" gang. As we look back on the year we spent there we can say with confidence that the Lord was with us. There was one episode in particular that made that evident to us. My responsibility was to keep the church clean in exchange for the apartment.

One day I was working with some youth that were helping me clean. We were all inside the building and the door was locked. I was busy cleaning when a knock came at the door. I didn't hear it but one of the teens did. He opened the door and two men were there. They said they wanted to see the pastor, so he brought them to me. Now alone with them they began to talk about the Bible in strange ways.

One man began to talk about how the apostle Paul buffeted or disciplined his body. Then something very strange took place. He drew back and clenched his fist. I was startled to say the least. Then he swung and punched himself on the cheek. Next, he made a fist with his other hand and hit the other cheek. He repeated the action a couple of times and his face began to bleed. Needless to say I was scared. I had never seen anything like this but what happened next was even more bizarre.

Suddenly the man flipped on his hands and began to run back and forth in the room on his hands. The room was long and narrow and I was quite nervous. I didn't know what to do but then instinctively cried out to God. Lord, I need power from above. Then it happened. I could feel power and boldness come upon me. I instructed the man to stop what he was doing and to sit down. To my surprise he did. Both the men were seated and like children they listened as I spoke of the gospel. When I was done I bid them farewell and they quietly left. I had never felt God's power like that before.

That was my first experience with the demonic. It would not be my last. I went back to my apartment a different person. Not only had I been made aware of the powers of darkness, but also the power of God. That day was preparation for an even more difficult day to come a few years later in my next place of ministry.

Dear Lord, thank you for revealing your power in me. I pray that you deliver us from the evil one. Assure us that in our time of need we can cry out to you and you will hear us. My prayer is for anyone who is struggling with defeat, let them know you have promised victory. Help us to learn how to resist the devil and draw near to God. Grant us the joy of seeing those in the bonds of Satan set free and bring glory to your name.

Thought: Be aware that we are not fighting intellectual battles but spiritual battles. Do you have loved ones or acquaintances that seem impossible to get through too. Pray for the power of God to be evident in your life. Be sure you have on the armor of God so you are able to stand against the schemes of the devil (Ephesians 6:10-15).

Personal Reflection:

Temple Baptist Church

*Now the Evangelical Spanish
Baptist Church*

CHAPTER 11
The Next Step

> **Delight yourself in the LORD, and he will give you the desires of your heart. Commit your way to the LORD; trust in him, and he will act. (Psalms 37:4-5 ESV)**

    I was grateful for the opportunity at Temple Baptist, but desired to get into some kind of pastoral ministry. Often I would check the student bulletin board at Moody to see what openings might be out there. One day there was a posting for a Youth Pastor position at the Meadow Lane Baptist Church in Hammond Indiana. I took the information down and made the call. The pastor at the time was Robert Chidister. I contacted him and set up an interview. Included in the process was attending a Sunday morning service and meeting with church leaders.
    The facility was wonderful. I would have a beautiful office with a door to the secretary's office. The pastor's office was on the other side. They had a great area dedicated to youth and I was excited about working there. The day went well and they told me a meeting would be held in a couple of weeks and I would know if I got the position. I

couldn't wait. I sensed the Lord was calling me there and I was ready. When I got back to Temple Baptist and caught up to the pastor I told him I would be leaving to accept the position at Meadow Lane. Then I began packing some of my things for the office.

A few days later I drove back to Hammond and went to the church door. It was locked and I rang the bell. The janitor let me in and I explained I had some of my belongings to drop off at my new office. He seemed a bit bewildered and reminded me the current Youth Pastor had not fully vacated the office. I assured him that was fine with me, I just wanted to get a head start on moving. I'm not sure if the pastor was in the building when I came or if the church secretary called him. He was surprised to see me and reiterated that the vote had not taken place yet.

I told him how excited I was about the position and was sure I was going to be hired. He was gracious and assured me the interview went well but he could not be sure of the outcome. Never-the-less he allowed me to move my items in. After unloading and checking the facilities more fully, I left and returned to Chicago. A few days later I received a call telling me the vote was positive and I gladly accepted the offer. By the grace of God one of the members had a contact who owned half a duplex. Now we had the position and a place to live. We were about to enter a four and a half year adventure of ministry.

I served under two pastors during my years there. It was here that I began to preach when the first pastor resigned and a search was made for a new pastor. This was a great learning experience. I discovered as I did in the Dale Carnegie Class that despite struggling with some language skills God was pleased to use me in pastoral ministry. To God be the glory.

> *Lord, I can honestly say you have given me the desires of my heart. As I look back over the years I rejoice that you have been pleased to use me. I thank you that in your sovereignty you judged me faithful, appointing me to your service. I praise you and glorify you that you have been pleased to use me in your service (1 Timothy 1:12).*

Thought: Have you discovered that God is pleased to use you for His glory? Whatever your weakness may be, there is no one who is outside of the scope of being used by the Lord. Each of us has been given a spiritual gift and with that gift a calling. Are you overwhelmed that the God of the universe has a call on your life? Have you felt the joy of moving forward in faith and discovered that "The steps of a man are established by the LORD, when he delights in his way;" (Psalms 37:23 ESV).

THE NEXT STEP 53

Personal Reflection:

Meadow Lane Baptist Church

Chapter 12
Learning To Ask

> **Ask, and it will be given to you; seek, and you will find; knock, and it will be opened to you. For everyone who asks receives, and the one who seeks finds, and to the one who knocks it will be opened. Or which one of you, if his son asks him for bread, will give him a stone? Or if he asks for a fish, will give him a serpent? If you then, who are evil, know how to give good gifts to your children, how much more will your Father who is in heaven give good things to those who ask him!**
> **(Matthew 7:7-11 ESV)**

As a youth pastor one of my roles was to open up the service and give announcements. This was in the seventies and almost everyone wore a suit to church. I only possessed one suit. I knew that the congregation would soon catch on to that. Not having the resources to go out and buy another one I prayed," Lord could you supply me with a second suit."

Shortly after that one of the parents of two children in my youth group asked me a question following the morning service. "Would you mind if I asked you your suit size?" she said. While that is not the kind of question you would expect to hear on a Sunday morning, I remembered my request. Upon hearing my suit size she invited me to come to her house after the evening youth meeting. She said someone had given her a suit that might fit me.

Arriving at the home I was shown an expensive suit that her neighbor had given to her. He had recently had a struggle with cancer and had lost a considerable amount of weight. It was his desire that someone who was serving God might be given it. I was shown to a room to try the suit on. It was a perfect fit. I had never owned such a fine outfit.

When I came out of the room everyone realized how nice it looked on me. The host then asked a favor. She wondered if I would go to her neighbor's house while wearing the suit so he could see it on me, and I could say thanks. I was more than glad to oblige.

We knocked on the door and both the husband and wife answered. The man was glad to see me in his suit. After initial greetings we were invited in. The women went to the living room to chat, and the gentleman led me to the master bedroom. Once there he opened up a large double-doored closet. It was filled with suits. He started taking out one after another. I think with the suit I was wearing it came to thirteen suits.

As I was loading the suits into my car I was reminded of a simple request. "Lord, can you supply me with a suit?" That occasion was the beginning of a life of many events that revealed to me how much God is involved in the lives of His people. James tells us "You do not have because you do not ask," (James 4:2). The request was quite small in the scheme of things. The answer displayed the glory of God, and that is why I tell the story.

After coming home with a car full of suits I realized I had been blessed beyond measure. I also knew God had not blessed me without the expectation that I would be a blessing. I got on the phone and called a couple of friends to see if they might need a suit or two. Their first response was, "Where are you going to get suits from?" How I enjoyed telling the story of God's abundant provision. We rejoiced together at the goodness of the Lord.

As you might expect I could not stop talking about the marvelous grace of God. One Sunday when getting dressed for church I realized my shoes were not nearly as nice as my suit. They had not looked as bad with my old suit but now it was obvious, I needed a new pair. So, I prayed, "Lord, I've got all these nice suits, do you think you could supply me with a pair of shoes?" What do you think? Tomorrow we will see what God did.

Dear Lord, how grateful I am for the many times you made it clear you are involved in the life of your Children. Thank you for the many wonderful answers to prayer I have experienced in life, and I pray that everyone reading this might be emboldened to ask as you have invited them to do.

Thought: Jesus tells us "whatever you ask in prayer, believe that you have received it, and it will be yours" (Mark 11:24). We may not have a total grasp on the wonder of this verse, but my experience has been that those who ask with the right motive get answers. Start praying and sharing when it is clear that "The Lord has heard your prayer."

Personal Reflection:

Chapter 13
He Is Able To Do Above All We Ask Or Think

> **Now to him who is able to do far more abundantly than all that we ask or think, according to the power at work within us, to him be glory in the church and in Christ Jesus throughout all generations, forever and ever. Amen.**
> **(Ephesians 3:20-21 ESV)**

One Sunday, shortly after receiving the suits mentioned in yesterday's devotional as I was getting dressed for church. I realized my shoes were not nearly as nice as my suit. They had not looked as bad with my old suit but now it was obvious, I needed a new pair. I am not sure of my prayer that day but was sure of the need. I was confident of the Lord's provision.

Monday, I got a call from one of the members. "Promise me you won't get mad, he said." I was startled and replied, "I'm sorry, what do you want me to do?" "Promise me you won't get mad" He replied. "Get mad" I inquired? "Yes, promise me you won't get mad." "Okay, I promise you I won't get mad." Then he quickly added, "Son those shoes you wore Sunday were shabby."

I explained to the caller that that was the only pair of dress shoes I owned. He let me know that was what he was thinking, and he was going to pick me up and take me to the local shoe store and buy me a new pair, and that is just what he did. You can bet I have told this account many times as I reflect upon the greatness of God.

Jesus said to "ask" and promised that if we do, we will "receive if we have faith" (Matthew 21:22). I do not understand everything about asking and receiving but this I know, God hears us when we ask, and I have had enough answers to be encouraged to keep on asking. To some these events are little things. To me it is the assurance that God hears our prayers.

Just when I thought it could not get any better, one more incident happened. Sometime after I was given the suits and shoes, a businessman, who attended the church approached me after the service. In the course of conversation he mentioned that he went through his wardrobe yearly and thinned out much of his clothing. In particular he got rid of his old ties replacing them with a new batch.

He asked if I would like to have them. I accepted his offer, and he brought them to me a week or two later. So now the Lord had provided suits, shoes, and ties.

What is interesting is I did not pray for the ties. I knew I could use a little more variety but had not given it much thought. But I had told the story of God's provision of suits and shoes to whoever would listen. I have discovered that the more you tell the story of God's glory in your life, the more stories you have to tell. Suits, shoes, and ties may not seem like much, but they are stories that go beyond coincidence. They demonstrate we serve a loving heavenly Father who is interested even in the smallest details of our lives.

When you share stories of God's blessings in your life you find the door opens up to share your faith. When the Lord healed the demon possessed man in Mark five, he wanted to go with Jesus but was instructed to:

"Go home to your friends and tell them how much the Lord has done for you, and how he has had mercy on you" (Mark 5:19).

There are some folks who have never seen the workings of God in their lives. I once had a man tell me he did not believe in God. I asked if I could tell him a story. After hearing it I asked if I could tell another. I told a number of events in which God had been actively involved in my life. After some amount of conversation he stated, "You have a connection with God."

Just a few moments earlier he said he didn't believe in God, now he acknowledged Him. So, it is when you tell others, how much the Lord has done for you.

> *Dear Lord, how many times you have made it clear you do far more than we are able to ask or think. Even when we do not recognize the need you make provision. As an earthly father wants to bless his children, so it is with you. The difference is you know our needs perfectly. Sometimes it is a material need, other times it is a spiritual need but never are you unaware. Let us bask in the abundance of your loving grace.*

Thought: Jesus invites us to pray. James says we have not because we ask not (James 4:2). It is possible to have selfish motives. But it is also possible to desire the glory of God. Start praying and sharing when it is clear that "The Lord has heard your prayer."

Personal Reflection:

Chapter 14
Deliverance From The Demonic

> Put on the whole armor of God, that you may be able to stand against the schemes of the devil. For we do not wrestle against flesh and blood, but against the rulers, against the authorities, against the cosmic powers over this present darkness, against the spiritual forces of evil in the heavenly places. Therefore take up the whole armor of God, that you may be able to withstand in the evil day, and having done all, to stand firm.
> (Ephesians 6:11-13 ESV)

One day a man came by the church I was serving at while in Hammond Indiana. He was encouraged by his family to visit me in hopes of helping him. He was suffering from severe depression, and it seemed personality issues. It was clear to me he had deep rooted spiritual issues. He was a very large man and many of his mannerisms made me nervous. I suspected there was demonic involvement. I spoke to him about some scriptural principles but felt I was getting nowhere. He especially seemed to have a reaction when I brought up the subject of Jesus.

I shared the encounter with another student at Moody Bible Institute and he was willing to help me with the individual. However we both felt ill prepared for the encounter. At that time one of the professors at Moody had written a book titled "Angels Elect and Evil". We made an appointment with Dr. Dickason seeking advice concerning how to work with the man. He was gracious and gave us some pointers. He felt it wise that we did not try to deal with the individual unless we were both present.

Having set a meeting time at the church we began to question the man to gather information. In the course of the conversation we often used the name of Jesus. It was not long before the mention of the name caused him to become highly agitated. We definitely felt we were dealing with the demonic. We asked many questions and discovered that he had been regularly seeing a fortune teller. Having become convinced this was his connection to demonic spirits we used the term "in Jesus name" all the more.

Then something happened. His voice changed and in a deep angry tone he cried out, "Stop using that name." We were both shaken by the voice and started to command him to say, "In Jesus Name." We were beginning to fear for our own safety, as he was a very large man and could easily overcome both of us. We brought the level of intensity down and were asking a series of questions trying to gain some information about the fortune teller. That is when we discovered that she had given him a record and had instructed him to listen to it.

That was the connection we were looking for! "Where is the record?" we asked. He told us it was in the trunk of his car. Soon we were in the church parking lot. Opening the trunk of his car he produced the record and gave it to us. We handed it back and told him "In the name of Jesus to break it in half." Here there was a man probably weighing over two hundred fifty pounds who could not break the record. He was trying to snap it in two but was shaking violently and screaming "I can't." We started screaming back, "In Jesus Name, break the record."

A spiritual battle was taking place. Two opposing forces were at work, messengers of the Lord and one enslaved by Satan. Neither side was quitting. We knew we were in spiritual warfare. Over and over we commanded, "In Jesus name we command you to break the record". Then it happened, the record broke. But more than that, an immediate change came over the man. He went from out of control, to calm and under control. We had just witnessed a man set free. The whole atmosphere changed. We could say the name of Jesus and there was no hostile reaction. We destroyed the remains of the record. Having prayed with him we then gave strict warnings not to visit the fortuneteller again.

> *Dear Lord, we have often failed to see or recognize the action of Satan in the lives of people. Yet we are told to be sober-minded and watchful. The devil is trying to confuse and destroy. Often our first reaction is to seek a medical cure for a spiritual problem. Forgive us for not seeing the need to pray and realize that our victory is in the Lord Jesus. "Let us not forget the devil is still seeking someone to devour" (1 Peter 5:8).*

Thought: Have we become so sophisticated that we have forgotten we are in spiritual warfare? While we do not want to see a demon in every corner we must not fail to recognize the involvement of demonic activity in our world. Let us be fervent in prayer. Let us also guard what we watch and where we go. Some things are wrong and dangerous. The devil is still active in this world. The name Satan means opponent or adversary. Let us not give the devil any opportunity (Ephesians 4:27). If you believe the Bible, pray and resist, seeking spiritual help is needed.

Personal Reflection:

Chapter 15

A Reason To Rejoice

> **Just so, I tell you, there is joy before the angels of God over one sinner who repents."**
> **(Luke 15:10 ESV)**

> **Precious in the sight of the LORD is the death of his saints.**
> **(Psalms 116:15 ESV)**

It has now been many years since the obituary in this devotional was written, yet the joy it brings to my heart is inexpressible. It might seem odd that an obituary could bring joy but after reading it I think you will discover why.

While at Meadow Lane Baptist one of the youth in my group shared that her parents were having some struggles. I decided to meet with them and in the process they both came to the Lord. They served Him faithfully until their death.

When the husband Nelson passed away his wife Naomi wrote his obituary. It touched my heart. I hope it touches yours also.

IN LOVING MEMORY OF NELSON KEITH BROWN Born: August 13, 1927, Died: August 20, 2001, Nelson went to work every day he worked. If there was a time he missed, it was because of a death. He taught himself electricity and planned all outlets and electric in our home. He died a horrible death from asbestos poisoning. He was the father of two chosen children and one I had. Theodore K. Brown, Susan Hancock, and Janice Brown. Theodore and Janice are deceased, Susan lives in Melbourne, FL. He received Christ in his heart in July 1976 as I the same from Pastor Sal Roggio. Our daughter Susan had been praying for us. Lord, thank you for giving Nelson to me to be my husband. Love, Naomi

Here is a teenage child praying for her parents. From there a simple visit takes place and her parents confess Jesus Christ as Lord. From that time on Christ is center stage in the household.

Nelson died many years after he came to know Christ as Saviour. From that time in 1976 both he and Naomi served the Lord. While we crossed paths a few times over the years I was surprised and honored to know that I was mentioned in the obituary. I was especially pleased to be reminded that one of the teens in my youth group was praying for her mom and dad. There surely was rejoicing in heaven that a husband and wife came to Christ and served him for the remainder of their lives. But more than that, there was the blessedness of a daughter who lived a shared faith with her parents. When her mother passed away in July of 2016 her daughter wrote these words,

A wonderful mother and a terrific mother. You will be sorely missed. But I look forward to one tremendous family reunion one day in the presence of our Lord Jesus Christ. Love you, Mom. Susan, August 5, 2016

My wife Nancy and I look forward to that reunion also. When we received word of Noami's home going we wrote these words in the book of remembrances.

Nancy and I share fond memories of Naomi. She was a wonderful caring person. She was clearly in love with Jesus Christ as Lord and Savior. Naomi will be missed on earth but has been welcomed into heaven to be with her Lord. We look forward to that day of grand reunion when we will see her again along with all who have put their trust in Him. May God's grace be upon all who mourn her loss.

What blessed memories. If God Himself rejoices in one person coming to salvation, let us rejoice also. Be encouraged that the Lord is pleased to use you in telling others of our Lord and saviour. And on those occasions that there is a response you will rejoice also.

> *Dear Lord, might we be found faithful in sharing our Saviour the Lord Jesus Christ. Grant us the joy of seeing a loved one, friend, neighbor or acquaintance come to faith and become a child of God. Let us never become complacent but rather fully convinced that Jesus is the way the truth and the life and may we share in the rejoicing that takes place in heaven.*

Thought: Just as Susan saw that the need of her parents was Jesus the Saviour, do you see Him as the answer to the problems of mankind? Do you long to be used by God in such a way that a life is changed. Are you looking for a grand reunion and maybe just one person there who will say, thank you for sharing Jesus. Do you proclaim as Paul, For I am not ashamed of the gospel, for it is the power of God for salvation to everyone who believes, to the Jew first and also to the Greek (Romans 1:16 ESV).

Personal Reflection:

CHAPTER 16

A DIVINE APPOINTMENT

> **So Philip ran to him and heard him reading Isaiah the prophet and asked, "Do you understand what you are reading?" And he said, "How can I, unless someone guides me?" And he invited Philip to come up and sit with him.**
> **(Acts 8:30-31 ESV)**

> **Then Philip opened his mouth, and beginning with this Scripture he told him the good news about Jesus.**
> **(Acts 8:35 ESV)**

WHILE A YOUTH PASTOR I wanted to take our youth group to Word of Life Camp. I was still a student at Moody Bible Institute and had heard the camp's founder, Jack Wyrtzen, speak and felt the camp would be a wonderful experience for our youth. There were a few obstacles to overcome. First was the distance. The camp was about 822 miles away, and the church had no vehicle. I began looking for a way to make it possible. After convincing the leaders of the church of the value of the trip I started to work on transportation.

I discovered that one of our families had a school bus that they were converting into a camper. It still had enough seats in it to carry the group of teens and a couple of leaders. I shared the vision, and they allowed us to use the bus. In those days churches did not need drivers with special licenses to drive buses. We picked a week, signed up the youth, and traveled the many miles to the camp. It was a week to remember. Yet the best part of the trip was when we headed home.

When we got to Ohio the bus began to give us trouble. Soon we found ourselves on the side of the road. It was not long before the State Police arrived. Seeing our situation they arranged for a tow truck. They also called for backup cars. All the youth got a trip in a state police car to the repair shop for the bus. They thought it was really great. Meanwhile I was thinking about the situation we found ourselves in . Here we are with a group of teens a couple of hundred miles from home.

While the teens were having an adventure at the coke machine, not being particularly worried about our situation, I thought I would go in and get an assessment from the mechanic. As he was leaning over the bus, I am telling him about the camp we went to sharing some of the things that had taken place. It was at that moment that something amazing happened. The man became a little choked up. He told me that his wife had recently died. He said he got up that morning and asked God to show him a reason to live. It was a holy moment as I was able to share the hope of Christ. It was truly a divine delay.

The mechanic soon had the bus up and running, and we were on our way. There were other problems that came up later and we finally rented three cars to get everyone home. From that point on nothing seemed to be too difficult. It was clear that God had used the breakdown of a bus to help repair a broken person. God heard his cry and taught me about divine delays. What seems like a problem to us at times, is the grace of God being extended to another. God gives us the opportunity to share His love to a hurting person.

> *Dear Lord, As Philip was led to the Ethiopian Eunuch so that he might understand the Gospel, (Acts 8:26-40), I thank you for divine appointments. Thank you for answering the prayer of a man who cried out to you in pain. Remind us as a loving Father you delight in hearing the cry of your children.*

THE GOODNESS AND WONDERS OF THE LORD

> **Thought**: Have you ever been used by God to touch the life of another person in the midst of a delay? Is that when you discovered how much our Lord cares for the hurting and lost? There is an old hymn that is worth becoming familiar with. The title is, "Does Jesus Care?" I have included the first and last verse. It speaks to the truth of this account. May the words be an encouragement to you today.

1) Does Jesus care when my heart is pained
Too deeply for mirth or song;
As the burdens press, and the cares distress,
And the way grows weary and long?

Refrain: O yes, He cares- I know He cares!
His heart is touched with my grief;
When the days are weary,
the long nights dreary,
I know my Savior cares.

4) Does Jesus care when I've said goodbye
To the dearest on earth to me,
And my sad heart aches till it nearly breaks—
Is it aught to Him? Does He see? [Refrain]
Author: Frank E. Graeff (1901) (Public Domain)

Personal Reflection:

CHAPTER 17

PASTOR, DO YOU HAVE A NEED?

> **And without faith it is impossible to please him, for whoever would draw near to God must believe that he exists and that he rewards those who seek him.**
> **(Hebrews 11:6 ESV)**

> **Oh, fear the LORD, you his saints, for those who fear him have no lack!**
> **The young lions suffer want and hunger; but those who seek the LORD lack no good thing.**
> **(Psalms 34:9-10 ESV)**

While on staff at Meadow Lane Baptist Church, I graduated from the Moody Bible institute. There was no tuition at Moody, and I used the G.I. bill income to cover our living expenses. Earlier I was living in the basement part of Temple Baptist church in exchange for serving as the church janitor. Now things changed when I moved to Hammond Indiana.

I started to attend Trinity Christian College to pursue my bachelor's degree. I was paying for college out of pocket and also, we were renting half a duplex to live in. Money was tight but our confidence was in the Lord.

My college bill was paid in installments and one week a bill was due for three hundred dollars. While we were very frugal with our resources we had come to a point where we did not have enough cash to make the payment. The bill was due on a Monday morning, and we prayed that God would provide our needs. We told no one about our dilemma but felt that the Lord had brought us this far and were confident we were in His will and our needs would be met.

Sunday came and I had a sense of anticipation as we headed to church. The service went on as usual and nothing out of the ordinary happened. We went home a bit bewildered because we had felt that the need would be met. The day passed quickly, and it was time for the evening service. When we arrived at the church one of the ladies approached me and wanted to ask me a question.

"Sal" she said, "do you have a need?" I said in effect, "We have a roof over our heads and food in our stomachs, we are doing ok." She replied, "Shut up Sal and tell me what you need." I meekly said "Well I do have a problem. I have a school bill due for three hundred dollars on Monday and I don't have the money to pay it." "I thought so," she said."

She reached in her purse and pulled out some bills adding up to exactly three hundred dollars. Then she told me a story. She said the Lord had caused her to wake up in the night before church on Sunday and placed in her mind that we had a need. As a result she approached a number of people in the morning service and told them of the event and collected money for us. As you might have figured out the sum came to exactly three hundred dollars.

Through the years we have seen God's divine provision. It wasn't long after that, when a wealthy businessman in the church requested I visit him. He had taken an interest in me and wanted to help with my college expenses. I do not remember how much he contributed, but I do remember that all my college expenses were met. I have learned that when the Lord calls, he provides, as the scriptures remind us, **"The Just shall live by faith." Hebrews 10:38**

Through the years I have accumulated many accounts of God's divine provision. I have been overwhelmed by God's grace and goodness. Many others in scripture and life's experiences give testimony to this. "We truly can trust in the Lord with all our heart" (Proverbs 3:5).

Dear Lord, remind us that we start by trusting you for salvation. We discover that our life becomes one of faith. Now we are learning that there is nothing too hard for God. We are reminded of the words of Paul when he said, And my God will supply every need of yours according to his riches in glory in Christ Jesus (Philippians 4:19 ESV). What a great promise.

Thought: Have you learned the difference between needs and desires? Sometimes we are disappointed because we did not get what we prayed for. Scripture tells us "And this is the confidence that we have toward him, that if we ask anything according to his will he hears us. And if we know that he hears us in whatever we ask, we know that we have the requests that we have asked of him (1 John 5:14-15 ESV). One of the great gifts God gives His children is the gift of answered prayer. Have you a testimony of a time when you can say, "The Lord heard my cry?"

Personal Reflection:

CHAPTER 18

WHO WILL SET ME FREE?

> Be sober-minded; be watchful. Your adversary the devil prowls around like a roaring lion, seeking someone to devour. Resist him, firm in your faith, knowing that the same kinds of suffering are being experienced by your brotherhood throughout the world
> (1 Peter 5:8-9 ESV)

AFTER ALMOST 6 YEARS as a youth pastor I heard of a church in Illinois looking for a pastor. After preaching a sermon and spending a Sunday there I was given the call to become their pastor. Needless to say, I was excited. After a short time the church began to grow. I was excited about what God might be doing. Then something strange began to happen.

One Sunday as I started to preach my mind began to fill with all kinds of cursing. I had been raised in a home during my teenage years where cursing was not uncommon. My four years in the Navy brought me in touch with many who saw foul language as a way of expressing oneself. Yet I had never picked up the habit. As a young child I had heard God's name taken in vain and was afraid that God himself would bring judgment on me for such action. Yet here I was standing behind a pulpit preaching from the Bible while my mind was filled with vile words.

That week I went to the church building to pray for relief. The more I prayed the more vile my thoughts became. I opened my Bible and began reading from Romans 7.

...I do not understand my own actions. For I do not do what I want, but I do the very thing I hate. Now if I do what I do not want, I agree with the law, that it is good. So now it is no longer I who do it, but sin that dwells within me. For I know that nothing good dwells in me, that is, in my flesh. For I have the desire to do what is right, but not the ability to carry it out. For I do not do the good I want, but the evil I do not want is what I keep on doing. (Romans 7:14-18 ESV)

That's what is happening to me, I said to myself. God help, I cried, deliver me. I did this a few times, yet relief didn't come. It was with fear that I began preaching the next Sunday. Would these awful thoughts return? What if I became confused and actually said one of these foul words from the pulpit? How could a man of God be so vile? Am I even fit to be a minister?

Defeated and tired, I returned to the church during the week. Maybe if I read the passage over and over, I would get to the truth of it and find relief. Once again, I went through Romans seven.

Now if I do what I do not want, it is no longer I who do it, but sin that dwells within me. So, I find it to be a law that when I want to do right, evil lies close at hand. For I delight in the law of God, in my inner being, but I see in my members another law waging war against the law of my mind and making me captive to the law of sin that dwells in my members (Romans 7:20-23).

Yes, I get it. I am a sinful man. A man of unclean lips and a filthy heart. I concurred with the Apostle Paul as I read the words:

Wretched man that I am... (Romans 7:24).

But Paul was a great man of God. He seemed to describe a battle that he had won. I was going through one I was losing. My life was flashing before me. All the training and preparation to be a pastor, was that now to be a loss? Was I degenerate? Had I just thought Jesus was my Savior but never really experienced salvation? I answered my own question. No, I believed in Jesus, this I was convinced of. This is an attack of the evil one I must stand firm. In my mind I cried out;

...Who will deliver me from this body of death? (Romans 7:24 ESV)

Then I read the verse that followed.

Thanks be to God through Jesus Christ our Lord! So then, I myself serve the law of God with my mind, but with my flesh I serve the law of sin (Romans 7:25 ESV)

I supposed I would have to live with the problem. My mind was clear that I wanted to live for God, despite this awful sin nature. Thinking that would solve the problem I went home.

To my dismay the problem continued to plague me. I couldn't live with this condition, and I needed to find relief. I went back to the church crying out who will deliver me. Once again, I was reading Romans seven. I was hoping to get to the place where I could say thanks be to God through Jesus Christ our Lord.

As I cried out to God an inner voice said to me, "Why did you stop at chapter seven?" It occurred to me that each time I had prayed I was identifying with Paul's experience of defeat. But the word was "Why did you stop at chapter seven?" I quickly turned to chapter 8 where I read these words.

There is therefore no condemnation for those who are in Christ Jesus (Romans 8:1 ESV).

I am sure I read that verse before. The truth of what I was reading hit me. I had been condemning myself in the struggle, even to the point of questioning my salvation. But the passage clearly said I was not condemned. I started crying out aloud, "I am not condemned." I even dared to yell out, "Satan, God says I am not condemned. I am in Christ Jesus, and I am not condemned."

Then it happened. The torture was over. The words went and so did the darkness. The battle was over. Sometimes people ask if the struggle ever returns. That answer will have to wait for another day.

Finally, be strong in the Lord and in the strength of his might. Put on the whole armor of God, that you may be able to stand against the schemes of the devil. For we do not wrestle against flesh and blood, but against the rulers, against the authorities, against the cosmic powers over this present darkness, against the spiritual forces of evil in the heavenly places. Therefore take up the whole armor of God, that you may be able to withstand in the evil day, and having done all, to stand firm (Ephesians 6:10-13 ESV).

> **Dear Lord, thank you for giving us the tools to resist the devil. Thank you that the truth sets us free John 8:32. Just as Jesus used the word of God to resist the temptation of Satan, remind us that the word is available to us also. Help us to remember Satan is a liar but your word is true and grant us the victory.**

Thought: Have you ever felt you were in a losing battle? "Fear not", is the word from God. Satan is a liar. Don't go by what you feel but rather by what you know. The scriptures remind us that greater is He that is in us than he who is in the world. (I John 4:4) When you have a struggle go to the word of God. Memorize the passages that lead you to victory and above all remember, " There is therefore now no condemnation for those who are in Christ Jesus (Romans 8:1).

Personal Reflection:

Chapter 19
Tammy

> **Have you not known? Have you not heard? The LORD is the everlasting God, the Creator of the ends of the earth. He does not faint or grow weary; his understanding is unsearchable. He gives power to the faint, and to him who has no might he increases strength. Even youths shall faint and be weary, and young men shall fall exhausted; but they who wait for the LORD shall renew their strength; they shall mount up with wings like eagles; they shall run and not be weary; they shall walk and not faint.**
>   **(Isaiah 40:28-31 ESV)**

When I first started preaching at Sauk Village Bible Church attendance was small. There was no one on staff but me. I had spent the years before as a youth pastor. As a result I thought I would plan something for youth by way of an activity. I contacted the school that was a short distance from our location and arranged to use a volleyball court. Then I spread the word. To my surprise a good group of teens showed up and we had a great night.

One young lady in particular was immediately noticed. She was small in stature, and it was obvious she suffered from a physical impairment. Her body was thin, frail and twisted. She struggled to walk let alone participate in the game. Despite her physical handicap she had a cheerful disposition and a smile on her face. After the evening, I spent a few minutes talking to her. She told me she was taking training to become a secretary. My first thought was she is going to have a challenging time finding a job with her limited motor skills.

It was then that the Spirit of God got a hold of me. The thought entered my mind, "Offer her a job at the church." We had no secretary, and our needs were growing. I was not sure she would be able to manage it but nonetheless made the offer. She was filled with smiles. Her name was Tammy and little did I know what a blessing she would be in the lives of so many people.

Tammy showed up for work the next week by way of a three-wheel bicycle. Churches were not handicapped accessible in those days and she had to navigate the ten or so concrete downward steps to get to the church office. It was a nervous moment as she slowly moved from step to step. But nothing seemed to worry her. She just kept smiling. Soon she would be known for her cheerful disposition. I do not remember her ever complaining.

Tammy worked for us for a few years. As time went by her health and strength deteriorated. No longer could she ride her bike to work. Her mother drove her, and she was now in a wheelchair. She was a trusting soul as I navigated the church steps with her seated in the chair. Still, she remained cheerful. As she further deteriorated her mother, Peggy, soon began to come in with her and they were known as secretary number one and secretary number two.

There came the time when Tammy could not work any longer. She had now become bedridden. When I would go to the house to visit her and her family one thing was obvious, Tammy never lost that smile and cheerful disposition. I have often thought about what the members of our church and I would have lost out on if I were not prompted on that first meeting to offer her a job. She was much more than a secretary, she was an ambassador for her Saviour, the Lord Jesus Christ.

> *Dear Lord, remind us of the value of each precious person you have created and called to serve you. Our limitations are eclipsed by your divine enablement. Let us realize that in your grace you choose to shine through us if we are willing vessels. Thank you for the witness and blessing brought to us by those who have been touched by your grace in a special way.*

> **Whom have I in heaven but you? And there is nothing on earth that I desire besides you. My flesh and my heart may fail, but God is the strength of my heart and my portion forever. (Psalms 73:25-26 ESV)**

Thought: Reflect on how many times you have been touched by someone who from all appearances is greatly limited, yet used in a special way by God. What is holding you back from serving the Lord with all your heart? Let us all, Serve the LORD with gladness! (Psalms 100:2 ESV).

Personal Reflection:

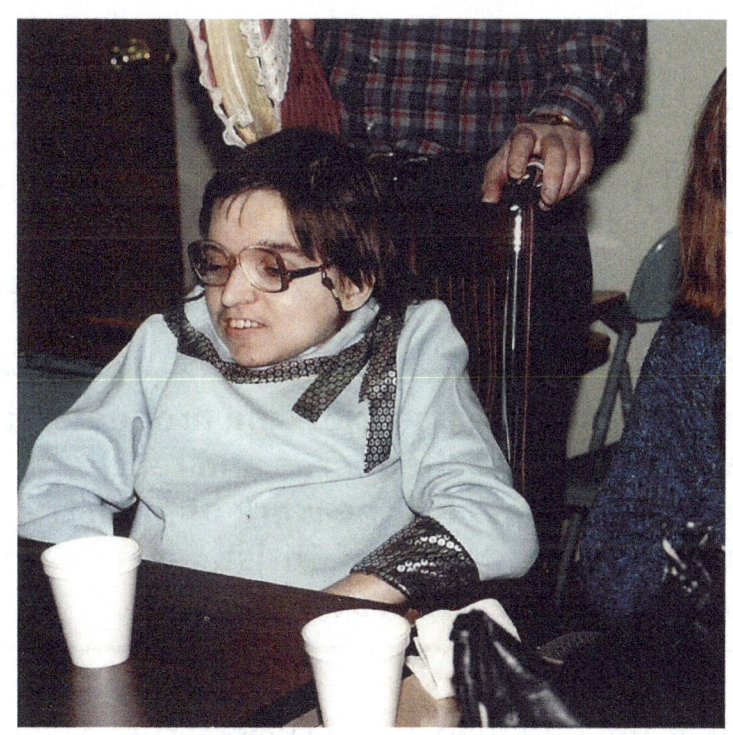

Tammy Bilyeu: Never without a smile!

Chapter 20
Ordination

> **And he gave the apostles, the prophets, the evangelists, the shepherds and teachers, to equip the saints for the work of ministry, for building up the body of Christ.**
> **(Ephesians 4:11-12 ESV)**

It was the period in which I was part of a Dale Carnegie Class that God confirmed in my heart His call on me to preach. (See day eight for details). I had no idea what would follow but learned that whom the Lord calls, he equips. The question was did anyone else share in that conviction concerning me?

It was while at Meadow Lane Baptist Church that the leaders decided to license me to preach. Though I was hired as a youth worker, I had been filling the pulpit every now and then and the congregation responded well to the messages. They were confirming God's call on my life. I also became part of the church leadership body. It was a time of growth and conformation.

One day a friend of mine told me of a church he preached at that was looking for a pastor. I was eager to investigate and when I did I was invited to be a candidate. I went there and it went very well. I was called to be their pastor. So we moved to Sauk Village Illinois, where I became the pastor of the Sauk Village Bible Church. I was excited.

By the grace of God the church began to grow. I do not remember how it came about but it was not too long before the subject of ordination came up. Being licensed is a local event. The leaders of the church recognize God's call on your life and make that decision. Ordination involved gathering a group of seasoned pastors to examine you. There you present a statement of your beliefs and answer any question the council may ask. If they sense you are truly called and in line with the scriptures they recommend that the congregation ordain you.

As wonderful as that is, have you ever considered the calling of God in your life? The Bible reveals that all believers are called in one way or another. Some are called to occupational ministry; but all are called to serve the Lord though in varying capacities. The Bible indicates that all Christians have been given one or more spiritual gifts. In that sense all are ordained to serve the Lord. You do not need a ceremony but simply a desire to be used by God.

To be sure, some are called to leave their employment and prepare for vocational ministry. But all are called to full time ministry in the sense that we are named "Ambassadors" (2 Corinthians 5:20). We all are called to represent our Saviour to a dying world. No believer has been overlooked.

Leaders are called "to equip the saints for the work of ministry (Ephesians 4:11-12 ESV).

> *Dear Lord, May we never get over the fact that all who have put their faith in the Lord Jesus Christ have become part of the family of God. Remind us that each has a role as a family member. Let no one consider their task of no consequence. Remind us that the "Body of Christ" consists of many members and that you have placed each one in where you want them.*

Thought: A pastor's role may be to encourage others in their role, but all believers are called to serve. All are significant in the cause of Christ. Do you know you have been called to action? Jesus tells us to "let your light shine before others, so that they may see your good works and give glory to your Father who is in heaven" (Matthew 5:16 ESV). The apostle Peter tells us to be "diligent to confirm our calling and election" (2 Peter 1:10). These instructions show how we serve as ambassadors. You can be sure the Lord will use you and you will know that in the Lord your labor is not in vain (1 Corinthians 15:58 ESV).

Personal Reflection:

98   THE GOODNESS AND WONDERS OF THE LORD

Chapter 21
Mr. Sunday School

> **For by the grace given to me I say to everyone among you not to think of himself more highly than he ought to think, but to think with sober judgment, each according to the measure of faith that God has assigned. For as in one body we have many members, and the members do not all have the same function, so we, though many, are one body in Christ, and individually members one of another.**
> **(Romans 12:3-5 ESV)**

When a new pastor comes to an established church you soon realize you are the new kid on the block. When I came to Sauk Village Bible Church, they had a Sunday School Superintendent who had served a long time in that capacity. Being a young pastor full of vision I began to suggest changes that might cause the Sunday School to grow. At first there was a sense of enthusiasm, but it wasn't too long before I felt opposition. The Sunday School started to grow but the relationship between the pastor and the superintendent became tense. I began to see the Superintendent as a roadblock to growth and felt the situation needed to change.

In this church they had an election every year for the officers. By this time, our relationship had become so difficult that the superintendent realized I did not want him to fill the position again. He stepped aside and someone else took the role that he occupied for those many years. The Sunday School grew but it seemed to many that it wasn't the same.

In the next couple of years, I had an opportunity to minister to the man's family. Some of the tension seemed to dissipate. People sensed the change and in the upcoming election of officers they asked if he could be placed as a candidate for Superintendent. I was willing and once his name was listed on the roster no one else would challenge him. As a result, once again he was in the place of service he loved to be in.

It wasn't long however before some of the old tensions arose. My patience was shorter than it had been the first time we worked together. One day after a difficult struggle over something I had shared in my vision for Sunday School, I went home with my mind made up that he had to leave that position. I was convinced it was not going to work. In effect it was a settled issue, I was going to ask for the resignation of this long-time volunteer.

The only remaining problem was how and when. Not wanting to make it worse than it was, I came up with what I thought would be a good solution. I placed a call to him and invited him to lunch. I didn't tell him why, but we set a date. On that day I drove to his house and picked him up. When he got into the car he began to speak with great excitement. "All these years I have been the Sunday School Superintendent and I have never had lunch with the pastor" he said. I told all my friends, "I am going to lunch with my pastor today".

I had never seen him so excited. The more he talked the more I realized I had a problem. I am taking him to lunch to ask for his resignation and he has told everyone he knows that His pastor is taking him out to lunch. Things were not going as planned.

Inside the restaurant Mr. Sunday school can't stop talking about all the years he has served. It is clear that this role means everything to him. It is also clear that he loved God and loved the children he had been responsible for. As I listened, I began to form the thoughts I might put into words concerning my frustration. Here is a summary of what I said.

I began the conversation by saying, "I have asked you to lunch today to help me solve a problem. He quickly replied, "Anything pastor, anything I can help with". I continued, "There is a man in our church that I know loves God. I am convinced he wants to be used by God and is being used by God. The problem is that for some reason or another it seems that we have trouble getting along and while he is a good worker he is hard to work with. If you had such a person in your Sunday School how do you think you might deal with it?"

The mood shifted and you could see that he was seriously considering the dilemma. "That's a tough one, pastor, I need to think about that." "So you understand my struggle." "Yes", he replied. For the next couple of minutes, you could sense he was wrestling with the problem. Then it happened. Tears began to flow from his eyes as he hung his head at the table. "I'm the man aren't I" he said. It was one of the holiness moments I have ever experienced.

An old, seasoned Sunday School Superintendent and a young new pastor at that moment experienced oneness in Christ. I began to appreciate his years of dedication. I saw the problem in a different light because I saw the man differently. We went on to serve together in the following years. In a special way God had taught me to give, "honor to whom honor is owed."

Dear Lord, teach us not to think more highly of ourselves than we should. As we are instructed let us give "respect to whom respect is owed, honor to whom honor is owed (Romans 13:7 ESV). By your grace let us carry only one debt in our relationships, that of loving one another (1 John 4:11).

Thought: In our enthusiasm to be used by God let us take care to honor fellow believers who have gone before us in faithful service. Remind us we are all gifted in different ways and not to allow our giftedness to cause us to be careless in our relationships. Bring to our minds your word when we find ourselves in difficult circumstances. "Love is patient and kind; love does not envy or boast; it is not arrogant or rude. It does not insist on its own way… (1 Corinthians 13:4-5). May we live our lives this way as we are taught, if I speak in the tongues of men and of angels, but have not love, I am a noisy gong or a clanging cymbal (1 Corinthians 13:1 ESV).

Personal Reflection:

Chapter 22

My God Is Bigger Than That

> **Now faith is the assurance of things hoped for, the conviction of things not seen.
> (Hebrews 11:1 ESV)**

Our Sunday School at Sauk Village was growing along with the rest of the church. The church building was not adequate and did not have the classrooms we needed. I had been watching the public schools and noticed that they had modular classrooms brought in when they needed additional space. The idea was great but the cost of a new modular for our sprouting church was too high.

Then I heard something that excited me. The schools were required by law to remove the buildings after they reached a certain age. It did not matter the condition of the classrooms. I saw that as a great opportunity. One day when one of our Sunday School leaders dropped by the church I mentioned the law and stated it was my intention to take a phone book and call every school in a short distance of our church and see if any had classrooms they planned to remove.

I grabbed a phone book and started dialing. The very first school I called said it was convenient that I did because they had three such buildings that needed to be removed. I asked when I could come by and see them not wanting to waste time or lose the opportunity. The response was right away. So I shot over to the school and could not believe what I saw.

Each building was equipped with two classrooms. They were fully outfitted with blackboards, carpet, and a girls and boys bathroom. To top it off, each had air conditioning units. I was elated and sat down with the superintendent to talk about the price. Imagine my joy when he told me they were only one dollar each. They simply wanted them removed. I made the deal and could hardly contain myself for joy.

Our next step was to find a way to move them approximately seven miles from where they were to where they needed to go. The logical action seemed to look up "House Movers" in the Yellow Pages. I found one not too far away and I and one of the church leaders drove to their office. With great excitement I told them of my purchase and wanted to know what it would cost to get them to our church property.

There were a couple of people in the office and they started to ask questions. Where were the buildings and where did they need to go. Then they asked how large the buildings were. I had measured the buildings while at the school so I quickly gave them the measurements. Each was 24 feet 6 inches by 36 feet. That's when the chuckling began. What's so funny I asked? One of the men said that I had bought a white elephant.

I didn't know what a white elephant was, so they were quick to explain. They said that in Illinois it was not legal to move a structure over the road that was over twenty-four feet wide. It would be impossible to get permits and I was going to get stuck with having to demo and remove three buildings. For a moment my excitement turned to gloom. I thanked them for their information and turned to leave the building. As I approached the door a muffled laughter could still be heard.

Suddenly without pre-thought I turned around and said in a clear voice filled with confidence, "My God is bigger than that, and we are going to move those buildings." Then I called the superintendent of the school and asked if I could come to speak to him again. In a few minutes I was back in his office and what took place in the next half-hour was nothing less than the hand of the living God. Yes, we did get permits. Truly our God proved himself able "to do far more abundantly than all that we ask or think," (Ephesians 3:20 ESV).

Dear Lord, how many times in life you have given us a glimpse of your glory. Circumstances sometimes may seem overwhelming, yet as we look back on life many times we find ourselves saying, "Only God!" Remind us in the difficult days of our life that you have many times shown that you are with us. Truly there is nothing too hard for the Lord.

Thought: Sometimes we need to be reminded that, " with God all things are possible." I have discovered that God loves to reveal His glory and cause us to worship Him. When at those times that require faith remind yourself that we worship the God who is able.

Personal Reflection:

Chapter 23

You Gotta Your Permits

> **Trust in the LORD with all your heart, and do not lean on your own understanding. In all your ways acknowledge him, and he will make straight your paths.
> (Proverbs 3:5-6 ESV)**

Having bought three modular buildings, and then being told we would never move them down the highway I headed back to the school. I was convinced that there was a way. I returned to the school officials office who had sold us the buildings and explained my dilemma. He thought for a minute and told me he was going to call the chief of police to see if he could help.

It was clear from the conversation that he had a working relationship with the chief. It was also clear the chief was Italian. He explained the issue to him. Then he handed the phone to me and said, "The chief wants to talk to you". I was expecting to go over the details concerning our problem, but the call went more like this.

"Hello" I said.

"Salvatore I'm Chief Rigittoni." (I have long since forgotten his real name, but there was no doubt he was Italian). Then he said, "You Italiano?"

"Yes sir" I replied.

"Sicilian?"

"Yes, Sicilian."

Then without missing a beat he said, "You gotta your permits"!

In one quick call our God proved again that "with God nothing is impossible". I reflected on that moment when I declared that my God is bigger than that. Now once again it was confirmed in my heart. Now to prepare to move the buildings. At first I thought of returning to the company I had gone to earlier. Then a thought came to my mind.

The same God who had just opened the door for us to move the building is able to make a way. I decided I was not going back to those who told me it couldn't be done. I felt the prompting of God to go back to the congregation and tell them what had happened. Then we would come up with a plan to move the buildings ourselves.

We were clueless but had mountain moving Faith. Those buildings were going to be moved, this we believed. And with that mountain moving faith we were ready for the task.

Dear Lord, remind us that we worship the God of the impossible. Let us reflect upon the times we had a glimpse of your glory. Encourage us when we pray that the first word is not the last. Remind us of the scriptures that say " The king's heart is a stream of water in the hand of the LORD; he turns it wherever he will (Proverbs 21:1 ESV).

Thought: Have you ever been told "It can't be done" yet in your heart you feel you must try. Trust in the Lord. Be reminded of the conclusion that Job came to at the end of his suffering, "I know that you can do all things, and that no purpose of yours can be thwarted" (Job 42:2 ESV). We receive nothing without faith, but when we put our hope in God we can see great things.

Personal Reflection:

It's easy to see why there was a width limitation

The Last Turn- The church property is one block up the street

Chapter 24

Mountain Moving Faith

> **Then the disciples came to Jesus privately and said, "Why could we not cast it out?" He said to them, "Because of your little faith. For truly, I say to you, if you have faith like a grain of mustard seed, you will say to this mountain, 'Move from here to there,' and it will move, and nothing will be impossible for you."**
> **(Matthew 17:19-20)**

We had just purchased three buildings. Having decided we would move them ourselves we began to put together a plan. One of the men in our church made his living by driving a Semi-trailer Truck. He owned his own and we thought he would be the best man from which to get advice. He informed us that we would need giant wood beams to go under the width of the mobiles, as well as to be cut for blocking. Not only would these have to be the width of the trailers or larger they would also have to be able to carry the load. These were nothing you could pick up at a lumber store. We did not know where to look, but God had already made provision for us.

After Sunday passed, our family needed to make a trip to the grocery store. On the way I passed the Chicago Heights Moose Lodge. We probably drove past the Lodge at least once a week as we shopped. But this time was different. There on the lawn of the lodge was a massive pile of giant timbers. I turned into the facility and found someone that was on the grounds. Where did this giant pile of timbers come from, I asked? The gentleman explained that a large old building had been torn down in Chicago and the lodge needed them for a building project. Then I popped the question. Do you need all of them? He replied no they had more than they needed.

I was a little afraid to ask what the large beams would cost but knew the question needed to be asked. In response to my question the man said we should get what they paid for them. I asked the next question, "What did you pay for them?" I was shaking inside expecting to hear a high price but to my surprise he answered we need $5.00 apiece. I was immediately overwhelmed with joy over the grace of God. Not only could we afford the price, but God had the beams shipped to about a mile from our church. Now to our next step.

Dan the owner of the Tractor trailer said we needed to find a lowboy trailer to rent that we could place the buildings on. Within a day we found one nearby. We shared what we were doing, and the man told us we could rent it for $50.00 a day. The words came back to my mind, "My God's bigger than that and we are going to move those buildings." I could hardly contain myself as I anticipated God's next provision. We were going to move those mobiles.

The last item we needed were jacks to evenly raise each building. I had a large mechanical jack I had been using for years. I called a number of rental places in the area, and none knew what a house jack was. I announced on the next Sunday we were looking for house jacks and asked if anyone in the congregation had one. We came up blank. The next time we met as a congregation I brought my jack to church. When I showed it to the congregation people said "That is not a house jack. That is a railroad jack." Railroads were a major employer in that part of the country. In a day or two we had all the jacks we needed.

We were ready to start. Soon we had the wood cut for blocking and the buildings jacked. One by one we back the trailer under each building. We moved one building a day. The police chief sent us an escort and had parked cars removed from the street, so we were not blocked. Two men were on the roof cutting tree limbs that might be a problem. The church van followed with flashing red lights. It was like a parade with people lining the streets. But one thing was for sure. "Our God was bigger than that" and three mobiles rolled down the road. Truly with God all things are possible.

> *Dear Lord, thank you for your testimony to the church and the community that you are truly able to do more than we could ever ask or think. May we glorify you through a holy boldness in the exercise of our faith. Give to us dear Lord wonderful memories of your involvement in our lives. When the way looks impossible, remind us that you are the Lord "who makes a way in the sea, a path in the mighty waters" (Isaiah 43:16).*

Thought: Are you facing something that looks far beyond your abilities? Something you don't feel you have the means to accomplish what lies before you. Have others told you it can't be done? Maybe this is a God moment where the Lord is saying "Step out in faith and see the glory of the Lord." Pray as the prophet Jeremiah did, 'Ah, Lord GOD! It is you who have made the heavens and the earth by your great power and by your outstretched arm! Nothing is too hard for you (Jeremiah 32:17).

MOUNTAIN MOVING FAITH 117

Personal Reflection:

All the cars removed from the street

Chapter 25

A Drive In The Snow

> **Humble yourselves, therefore, under the mighty hand of God so that at the proper time he may exalt you, casting all your anxieties on him, because he cares for you.**
> **(1 Peter 5:6-7 ESV)**

Feb 27, 1984 Chicago and the surrounding area had what was described as a Thundersnow.

Nancy was working at a nursing home and scheduled to work the 3-11 shift that evening. I told her I could get her there with no problem. We had just recently purchased a good used car which I considered snow worthy. Living in the Chicago area, we had many opportunities to drive in heavy snow and I was looking forward to taking my new used car out in the latest storm.

We started out at 2pm-which gave me 1 hour to drive just 5 miles. In my favor, or so I thought, the roads had already been plowed. However, getting out of our community had some challenges I hadn't considered. The main streets were plowed but the plows left high piles of snow at the end of each side street. I was not worried. I figured this car would have little trouble driving through the piles of snow. I approached the first pile. I gave the car some gas and attempted to plow myself through the snowbank. I crashed into the snow pile, but it was a struggle. The next plan was to shovel the high pile down enough to drive over it. Next corner I tried again; backed up and hit the gas. Bang. Again, I needed to shovel the pile of snow down. Finally, we were on the main road. But it took the entire hour to drive the 5 miles. Then of course I needed to drive back home and repeat my efforts again before 11pm. Since I had already cleared a path I felt the trip back to the nursing home would not be as difficult.

   I got there a little early, parked and waited for Nancy to come out when her shift ended. When she entered the car I started to drive. That's when we discovered one of the tires had gone flat. Maybe from the original trip when I was navigating exiting the side streets. Not a problem I thought, I know how to change a tire. I was only in my mid-thirties and liked challenges. However, when I opened the truck I found out my new car was missing something very important. The spare was there, and the jack was there, but the lug wrench which also served as the jack handle was missing. We were both tired and concerned about how we would get home in the storm.

For some reason I decided to leave Nancy in the car and began to walk down the street searching for a solution. There were trash cans on the side of the road, and I began to check them out. Who knows but I might find something that could solve our problem. As I am doing this I am praying for God's help to get out of the jam we found ourselves in. Not to mention how I felt as the husband that had failed to adequately prepare for his family. Yet even in this difficult moment I felt confident God was with me.

While looking around the trash containers to my surprise I saw something on the ground. It was one of those moments that seemed too incredible to believe. There on the ground covered with snow was a lug wrench. I scarcely could believe it yet was overwhelmed with joy. Picking it up I rushed back to the car hoping it would work on my lug nuts and jack. It did! I was filled with praise and thanksgiving. Soon the car was jacked, and the tire changed. By God's grace we were on the way home.

Dear Lord, Thank you for being forever involved in the affairs of your children. Over and over in life you have listened to the cry of your servant. There can be no other explanation than "The Lord heard my cry" (Psalms 116:1). What is so great is even in the smaller events of life you are there. Over and over you demonstrate to your children that you care and are truly the good Shepherd. I thank you that your word is true when you tell us "I will never leave you nor forsake you (Hebrews 13:5). Thank you for being my Heavenly Father.

Thought: Have you ever felt like you deserved what you got? How could I have been so careless? Yet in that entanglement of emotion you discover that your heavenly father cares for you. You are invited to cry out to Him even when you feel like a failure. Have you at last come to the understanding that our heavenly Father loves to embrace us with His Grace. Do not be afraid to cry out "Abba Father" (Galatians 4:6) which in effect Is crying out "Daddy, Daddy". The wonderful thing is that our heavenly Father responds. Let His embrace fill you with worship.

Personal Reflection:

Chapter 26

The Holy Spirit

> **But the fruit of the Spirit is love, joy, peace, patience, kindness, goodness, faithfulness, gentleness, self-control; against such things there is no law.**
>   **(Galatians 5:22-23 ESV)**

Many years ago I was asked to visit the home of a man who was struggling with alcohol. His family was part of our church fellowship and I think he had attended a few times. They were greatly concerned about how this habit had gotten control of him. I was glad to make the visit but was aware that many who struggled with this habit seem to have a difficult time gaining victory. I have not struggled with drugs or alcohol. But I recognize we all live in a spiritual battle and the devil is seeking whom he may devour (1 Peter 5:8).

The Bible tells us when we become believers, the Holy Spirit comes to live within us. In fact if we do not have the Holy Spirit living in us, scripture declares we are none of His (Romans 8:9). I remembered when pastoring in Illinois, one of the first people I met told me that he was formerly an alcoholic.

He went on to say while alone in his home he was watching a Billy Graham crusade on his television. He took the message to heart and at the time of the invitation went to his knees and asked Jesus to become his Lord and Saviour. After that he got up and did away with all his alcohol.

I saw a dramatic example of this after I visited the man struggling with alcohol. I affirmed his faith in Christ. Then I explained that God through His Spirit would enable him to say no to drinking. I was careful to reinforce the fact that he did not have to drink. As a believer God would give him the ability to stay sober. I left hoping he would have the victory. While I was certain God could free him from this habit I was concerned he might not fully believe it.

About a week went by and I thought it would be prudent to visit him again. I went to his home and started the conversation with mostly small talk. I was observing him to see if there were any telltale signs that he was still drinking. Finally I got to the question. I asked how he was doing and if he had anything to drink that week. He said he was doing fine and was not drinking. Then in a minute or two he hung his head and said, "I can't lie to you. I went out and bought a six pack a couple of days ago. I was saddened and asked what he did with it. I was expecting the answer would be I drank it.

I was prepared to exhort him and remind him that by God's grace he did not need to be a slave to sin. It was at that moment that the grace of God showed itself as he answered my question. I went out the other day and bought a six pack, he told me. When I got home I took one of the cans and opened it. As I put it to my lips to drink something happened. I became convicted and poured it down the drain. I was excited to hear that and was rejoicing in my heart. Then it occurred to me. There were five cans unaccounted for. Then came my next question.

What happened to the rest of the six pack? I was expecting He would have to confess that they were stashed somewhere. To my surprise he told me after he disposed of the first can, he reached for the other cans and one by one poured them down the drain. Then his eyes lit up and the volume of his voice increased as he cried out, "Man, is the Holy Spirit powerful." I can reply to that, "Amen yes He is!"

Let us never fail to tell people when they put their faith in Jesus they no longer have to be slaves to sin. We are able to have victory. We go from slaves to sin to slaves of righteousness. It is a matter of faith and obedience believing God is in us and with us. Listen to the words of Paul in Romans. "But thanks be to God, that you who were once slaves of sin have become obedient from the heart to the standard of teaching to which you were committed, and, having been set free from sin, have become slaves of righteousness" (Romans 6:17-18 ESV).

> *Dear Lord, we thank you that you sent Jesus into the world so that we might be able to receive forgiveness of sins. Thank you for asking the Father to send us another helper who is the Holy Spirit. We are encouraged in that we do not walk alone. Thank you that the Holy Spirit is helping us in our weakness and by his grace we can live a holy life (Romans 8:26). May we learn to live by faith in the power and promises of the Holy Spirit.*

Thought: Have you been living below your means? Have you tried to have victory in your own power? Cry out to God in your struggles and you will discover that God has made provision for you to be victorious. Then you will cry out, "Man is the Holy Spirit powerful".

Personal Reflection:

Chapter 27
Never Forsaken

> Why are you cast down, O my soul, and why are you in turmoil within me? Hope in God; for I shall again praise him, my salvation and my God.
> (Psalms 43:5 ESV)

Many wonderful things happened at my first pastorate. I had accepted the position with the goal of spending my life there. Often I was saddened by how many churches had pastors who only stayed for a few years than moved on to another ministry. But something else was happening. I'm not sure I fully understand what took place. The church was growing. We had added buildings. I started working on a master's degree. Our family had grown to 4 children. I dropped out of the master's program, but Nancy went to nursing school.

In the midst of it all, I became discouraged. My view of ministry did not line up with the way things are done in many church settings. I soon came to realize I didn't fit. I felt that the structure of the church was often counterproductive. My feeling was voting and structured meetings often pitted one believer against another. Along with that I struggled academically. I felt I was perhaps in the wrong calling. After a conversation with my wife, I decided to resign. The next couple of weeks were very difficult. While we were packing and preparing to leave, folks from the church would drop by to say farewell. We would all end up weeping. It was emotionally exhausting.

Next, we needed to have a place to go. I fully expected to make a change in careers. We returned to our two bedroom mobile home in Laurel Lake, New Jersey. We had put it up for sale when we left for Chicago some twelve years earlier. We had rented some of those years but now it was vacant. Thus in June of 1986 we headed back to New Jersey and moved our four daughters, us, and our dog into it. When we arrived Nancy took a nursing job, and I took odd jobs and then began to substitute teach. We went to the church where we attended before leaving for college, while also visiting other churches. But something was not right.

It wasn't long before I realized none of the things I was doing would satisfy. It was not who I was made to be and not what I was created to do. Sunday after Sunday I realized I was called to teach God's word. However, I did not want to step into the same kind of framework I had resisted. I mentioned to a few people my vision of church. To my surprise they were ready to join me in this pursuit. And so we started the Cumberland County Community Church. It has now been over thirty-five years. As I look back, I am amazed at what the Lord has done. God has continued to display His Goodness and Wonders.

The remainder of this devotional tells just a few of the stories of how God has helped us along the way. As the scriptures tell us, Jesus Christ is the same yesterday and today and forever (Hebrews 13:8 ESV). Even in a period of discouragement and confusion we discovered God in His faithfulness never deserted us.

Our first task was to find a meeting place. I knew the Millville Hospital had a large meeting room attached to it. I contacted the hospital and they agreed to let us use the space. But a week or so before we were to start they sent me a letter resending the offer. Now we were in a jam. We were prepared to start and had no place to meet. What were we to do?

I remembered that while in Illinois we had rented space from a public school. I thought I would give it a try. I called the board of education and made the request. They said I needed to meet three criteria. First I had to prove I was a fully ordained minister. That was easy having been ordained a number of years earlier. Second, I need to demonstrate the urgency of the need. I had the letter canceling the use of the hospital. Again, that was not a problem.

The third request stopped us in our tracts. They said I needed to be a member of the Millville Ministerium. I had met some of the pastors in town but was not part of the ministerium. The third demand could not be met. As I was praying about our situation it came into my mind to call the school board back. I ask if the third requirement was legal? How could they require me to be a member of the ministerium? They said they would call me back.

Within the hour I received a call from the School Board. They said they had found a building that was available for us to rent and meet in. I secured the landlord's information and the address of the place. It was an old building that had been converted into a church. Strange as it may seem we were told at one time it was a business called "Salvatore's Studio". I could only smile. And so a church was born.

> *Dear Lord, it is no wonder that the Words of David are loved by so many. He restores my soul. He leads me in paths of righteousness for his name's sake. Even though I walk through the valley of the shadow of death, I will fear no evil, for you are with me; your rod and your staff, they comfort me (Psalms 23:3-24 ESV). In the dark day you prove to be a shining light. Thank you for keeping your promises given in your encouraging words.*

Thought: Have you ever experienced a time of confusion and discouragement? The book of Proverbs reminds us: The crucible is for silver, and the furnace is for gold, and the LORD tests hearts (Proverbs 17:3 ESV). The death of a vision does not mean God is finished with you. As I experienced, the death of a vision did not cancel my calling but did change my direction. The promise of God is, The steps of a man are established by the LORD, when he delights in his way; though he falls, he shall not be cast headlong, for the LORD upholds his hand (Psalms 37:23-24 ESV). Even in times of confusion, put your hope in God.

Personal Reflection:

Our First Meeting Place

We Spruced Up The Front

The Back Needed A Little More Help

Chapter 28
A Title Deed From God

> **Oh give thanks to the LORD; call upon his name; make known his deeds among the peoples! Sing to him, sing praises to him; tell of all his wondrous works! Glory in his holy name; let the hearts of those who seek the LORD rejoice! Seek the LORD and his strength; seek his presence continually! Remember the wondrous works that he has done, his miracles and the judgments he uttered,**
> **(1 Chronicles 16:8-12 ESV)**

Having the provision of a building helped us become a little more established. The building was old and needed attention, but we were doing all we could to keep up with it. Growth was slower than we had hoped for, and some felt it was due to the building and location. We knew this was a beginning and not an ending.

Then we got a surprise. The Landlord told us he was selling the building, and we would have to vacate. We didn't have a written lease and so would have to find an alternative quickly. Yet we were still a small church without the sufficient resources to build. We did not even own a piece of land. What were we to do?

We started to look around for options. Having checked with other churches we found those options were limited. By chance it came to our attention that the local Elks lodge might be available. It only worked for Sunday mornings, but we could have smaller meetings in our homes. This did not solve the problem, so we started looking for land. Another problem existed. We would need to borrow the money to buy the land, but did not have the resources to build. Nonetheless our confidence was in God. Our conviction was He would lead and provide.

We started to worship in the Elks Lodge. Getting there caused us to pass a property that used to be an old chicken farm. It was run down with hundreds of feet of old chicken coops. One day while riding by with a friend I noticed a sale sign had been put on the land. We stopped the car, and I ran on to the property. It was a nice piece of land with a small house on it. I cried out with joy, this is it. This is where we will build the church.

Later I called the realtor and told him our intention. I asked him to call the owner and tell him we wanted to get the best price we could because we wanted to buy the land. I told him we were going to use it to do a great work for God. He told me he would talk to the owner. Later he called back and said the price was $68,000. The owner felt the price was fair since the house had neither a working septic nor water so he was selling it for land value. That was a lot of money for us and I asked him to call the owner back to see if he would reduce the price. "Remind him we want the land because we were doing a great work for God."

Later in the day he called back and said the price would not be reduced but the owner would give us the piece of land that was separated from the main lot when they had extended the road at the back of the property. "How big is it?" I asked. I was told about four hundred square feet. I went to City Hall and asked them what that little piece of land might be worth. Smiles went up in the office as they said, "Four hundred square feet is worth nothing". I thought for a moment and replied, "Everything is worth something" and I was going to buy the land and take the little lot across the street.

We signed the papers, put down a deposit and began the loan process to secure what we needed. Then it happened. The title company called and asked if we were getting both properties on the other side of the street. I told them I was only aware of the 400 square feet. The spokesperson said there was a problem. When the road was put in they deeded the 400 feet of land with a larger lot the seller owned.

The next step was to call the property owner and inform him the closing could not go forward until the discrepancy was cared for. Not wanting to postpone the sale and separate the little lot from the larger lot the owner said give them both lots. We now went from 400 square feet to about 10,000 square feet. That was large enough to be a building lot.

Soon we were busy. We got the well and septic working in the old house and cleaned it up. We subdivided it from the main lot and sold it for $58,000. The lot across the street sold for $10,000. Apart from miscellaneous costs, in effect we got the land for free. Next would come the buildings. God did so many wonderful things on our behalf it would take another 31-day devotional to cover them all. Perhaps we will try this again.

> *Dear Lord, how wonderful it is to know as we move forward in obedience and faith we can be confident that in our planning it is you who establishes our steps. (Proverbs 16:9) Remind us that we are never left on our steps established by you and you are still the God of wondrous deeds. Encourage us to tell of all your wondrous deeds.*

Thought: Have you ever considered if you told of all God's wondrous deeds in your life you would have a lot to talk about. A simple detail becomes a story of praise. Do not allow the world to silence you. Watch out for the details that will cause you delight in the Lord and sing His praise!

Personal Reflection:

Chapter 29
The Reality Of Humanity

> **Come now, you who say, "Today or tomorrow we will go into such and such a town and spend a year there and trade and make a profit"—yet you do not know what tomorrow will bring. What is your life? For you are a mist that appears for a little time and then vanishes. Instead you ought to say, "If the Lord wills, we will live and do this or that."**
> **(James 4:13-15 ESV)**

God has a way of reminding us how brief life on earth is. It is not that there are no warnings in the Bible but rather we are too preoccupied to seriously consider that fact. Moses, who lived to be 120 years old, wrote that for our length of life might be 70 or eighty Psalms 90:10. In reality no one knows when their end will come but the wise prepare for that time. Whenever I preach a funeral I am sure to include the gospel message. The scriptures are clear.

The Bible tells us "It is better to go to the house of mourning than to go to the house of feasting, for this is the end of all mankind, and the living will lay it to heart" (Ecclesiastes 7:2 ESV).

It is when we are faced with death that we become in many cases more open to the truth that "it is appointed unto man once to die, then comes the judgment" (Hebrews 9:27). The most tragic mistake a person can make is to be unprepared to leave this earth.

This truth was at the forefront in my thinking in 2014. I had been suffering pain in my chest for some time. After a catheterization, it was discovered that four of the arteries going to my heart were seriously blocked. I had tried a number of things in an attempt to correct the situation. It looked like I was making progress, but we soon discovered it was not sufficient. It was time for surgery.

I am grateful for the surgery. Yet I knew the seriousness of the matter. But what was so amazing to me was how calm I felt. I had asked Jesus to be my savior many years earlier. I believed the Bible account of Jesus' death on the cross for me. The scriptures made it clear that "if you confess with your mouth that Jesus is Lord and believe in your heart that God raised Him from the dead you will be saved" Romans 10:9.

How different life is when you realize that the life to come is better. Yes, it is nice to be loved. There will be sadness in separation. But even for those who are left behind I was reminded that "We do not sorrow as those who have no hope (1 Timothy 4:12). The fear of death was removed years ago. Since we all live with the surety of death, but much more we who know the Lord, live in the guarantee of eternal life.

So as I kissed my wife and was wheeled away I was calm. How sad that people live and die with no hope. Have you spent so much time in the now that you have lost perspective on eternity? I had no choice about being born. It was out of my control as to where I would be born. Many things that happened to me, whether good or bad, were not my doing. But one thing I am sure of, I have a bright future.

It was not hard for me to recognize my sinful heart. When the Bible told of the wages of sin I didn't need any convincing. When the offer of forgiveness and the promise of heaven was given to me I took it. I still don't know when I will die. I have passed the 70 mark and am halfway to eighty. Will I make it, who knows. But this I do know. When I die I will go to be with my Lord and Savior in Heaven.

That is why I could be calm as I faced surgery. Considering the shortness of life and the wonder of salvation, why anyone who has heard the gospel would not settle that issue is startling. To live for today is to miss out on the peace of God and the presence of God for eternity. What a tragedy.

Dear Lord, Thank you for the peace of God which surpasses all human understanding. Remind us we do know the future, but we are assured that You are our future. Let us continually confess the scriptures which tell us, But, as it is written, "...no eye has seen, nor ear heard, nor the heart of man imagined, what God has prepared for those who love him"—
(1 Corinthians 2:9 ESV) With that our Lord the reality of our humanity will dim in comparison

Thought: Are you so caught in the now that you have been blinded to eternity? I pray if you are, you will hear the words of Moses who cried out to God, "...teach us to number our days so that we may get a heart of wisdom" (Psalms 90:12 ESV). If you have never put your faith in the Savior, will you not decide right now? Tomorrow is not guaranteed.

Personal Reflection:

CHAPTER 30
THE 911 CALL

> Is anyone among you sick? Let him call for the elders of the church, and let them pray over him, anointing him with oil in the name of the Lord. And the prayer of faith will save the one who is sick, and the Lord will raise him up. And if he has committed sins, he will be forgiven.
> **(James 5:14,15 ESV)**

I have experienced a number of kidney stones in my life. Usually, I live with the pain until it passes. I also find myself praying for relief. One day I began to experience another stone. I did all I could to find relief. Plenty of liquids and eating the recommended foods was the usual process. And yes, prayer. However, as the days went by the situation worsened. It became so intense that I realized it was time to seek a doctor out.

I visited him, got some advice, and went home expecting in a couple of days it would pass. It did not and the pain was excruciating. Upon a return trip to the doctor he told me the stone had blocked my urinary tract and the stone would have to be surgically removed. I suggested I would like to wait it out longer. He suggested it could become life threatening and needed to be cared for quickly. Not wanting to, but with the encouragement of my wife, I agreed. That was on a Monday and the procedure was scheduled for Wednesday morning.

I am sure I was praying for relief but must admit it didn't occur to me to call the elders or let others in the church know about my condition. I simply went home and laid down on the couch groaning in pain and hardly able to move. By now I was willing to do anything to solve the problem. Suddenly there was a knock at the door. A preacher friend opened the door and came up to where I was. He told me God had told him to come and pray for me. While we were talking and before he prayed another knock came on the door. They too let themselves in, and it turned out it was the elders of the church. They also said that God had told them to come and pray for me.

I welcomed their prayers. The old preacher kneeled down and put his hand on my knee. The other men gathered around him. Then He began his prayer. "God" he said, "this is a 911 call". I was a little taken aback, I am in serious pain and the preacher is making a 911 call to God. It almost felt like he was joking. The others offered short prayers, and all wished me relief. Then they said goodnight and left. Nothing happened. I was still in serious pain and still anticipating the medical procedure on Wednesday.

I spent the next hour lying on the couch, coming in and out of sleep. Then I felt the urge to go to the bathroom. I had tried before, but the blockage was too much. But something was different. Something was happening in my body. I sensed the stone breaking up. I went to the bathroom and the crumbled stone passed from my body and I felt immediate relief. God in His mercy heard the 911 call.

The whole event was a surprise to me. I was in awe that the pastor and elders came having sensed the call of God. I was filled with thanks that God hears 911 calls. My faith increased on that day. Thanks to those who responded to the call and praise be to God. The next day I canceled my surgical procedure, and had a story to share.

> *Dear Lord, thank you for the evidence that you give that you care for us as a father cares for his children. I thank you for the faithful men who came in obedience to your prompting. In their obedience and your grace I found relief. Thank you for reminding me the prayer need not be eloquent but rather offered in faith. And thank you that the prayer of faith is still able to bring healing to the sick and honor to the Lord.*

Thought: Have you considered how much the Father cares for His children. While sometimes He goes through the storm with us, sometimes He takes us out of the storm. One of my favorite verses is found in the book of Jeremiah. Call to me and I will answer you, and will tell you great and hidden things that you have not known (Jeremiah 33:3 ESV). I invite you to accept God's invitation.

Personal Reflection:

Chapter 31

Prayer and Proclamation

> I will remember the deeds of the LORD; yes, I will remember your wonders of old. I will ponder all your work, and meditate on your mighty deeds. Your way, O God, is holy. What god is great like our God? You are the God who works wonders; you have made known your might among the peoples.
> Psalms 77:11-14 ESV

Prayer is both simple and complicated. This little devotional has been filled with testimonies of God's involvement in my life and others. Does God work in all believer's lives? Yes! The apostle Paul tells us to continue steadfastly in prayer. (Colossians 4:2) In another passage he tells us to pray without ceasing. (1 Thessalonians 5:17) This does not mean we are on our knees twenty-four hours a day, but it does means we live in constant awareness of, and are in communication with God.

Often, we are discouraged when we pray and do not get the answer requested. Sometimes God's purposes are different than ours. Even the apostle Paul prayed for relief from a struggle three times and God responded by giving him grace to endure. God says in Isaiah, "my thoughts are not your thoughts, neither are your ways my ways." (Isaiah 55:8) Different things can happen when we pray. We can pray out of the will of God, or ask with wrong motive. (Jame 4:3)

Then there is the issue of faith. The author of Hebrews tells us, "without faith it is impossible to please him, for whoever would draw near to God must believe that he exists and that he rewards those who seek him." (Hebrews 11:6 ESV) I have discovered with God nothing is impossible, but He always operates in the realm of His holiness.

Yet I have also discovered that the believer who is walking in the Spirit will see the hand of God in his life over and over. The accounts in this devotional are not greater than they are in the lives of most believers. But I have noticed something. Believers often fail to tell the stories of His grace and mercy. I think sometimes they may think they are trite. They are not. They are indicators of God's love for His children and his involvement in their lives.

Once on a teen retreat we were staying in a host home. All of a sudden panic hit as one of the girls declared she had lost her high school ring. She had just recently got it and was fearful of telling her mother it was lost. We had all the teens do a thorough search of the area of the home we were staying. They searched and searched but the ring could not be found. As we were all gathered together I thought it would help to pray. At the end of the prayer I saw a small trash can in the room. I suggested they check the can. "We already did," a couple of the youth shouted back. "Do it again," I said. I got the youth look that said "ok, but don't expect to find anything." As they turned the can upside down a sound occurred, the sound of the ring hitting the floor.

That evening turned into a teachable moment. The whole group had witnessed what had taken place and how God had answered our prayer. Each could go home and tell the story. These are the kind of accounts God gives of His love for us. This is how He displays His grace. Should we not tell the story often? You will soon discover the more you share the more you will have to share. Yes, your story is waiting to be heard.

As we close out this thirty-one day devotional, has your heart and mind been stimulated to recall the many times God has shown His active involvement in your life? These remembrances open the door to sharing your love for God. Get out a pencil and paper and begin to number the events that are a clear indication of the hand of God moving on your behalf. You will be surprised and filled with joy.

> *Dear Lord, thank you for the clear evidence that you are directly involved in the life of your saints. Thank you that we can say as the author of Hebrews declared, "The Lord is my helper." (Hebrews 13:5) Thank you that you hear our prayers and do more abundantly than all we can ask or think. (Ephesians 3:20) Dear Lord, may we bask in your love, the love of our heavenly Father for His children.*

Thought: Bless the LORD, O my soul, and forget not all his benefits...(Psalms 103:2 ESV). Thus we are instructed in scripture. Yet it is possible as we travel through life to forget. Many in Israel and in the New Testament did. But let us not be those who join the ranks of the many. How do we keep from forgetting, but repeating the stories of God's involvement in our lives. Think of one story of God's involvement in your life that your could share with someone. Then start looking for who that someone might be. Trust God to open the door and go through it.

Personal Reflection:

Made in United States
Orlando, FL
30 June 2024